Microservices Development Cookbook

Design and build independently deployable, modular services

Paul Osman

BIRMINGHAM - MUMBAI

Microservices Development Cookbook

Technical Reviewer: Matt McLarty
Commissioning Editor: Merint Mathew
Acquisition Editor: Alok Dhuri
Content Development Editor: Rohit Kumar Singh
Technical Editor: Ruvika Rao
Copy Editor: Safis Editing
Project Coordinator: Vaidehi Sawant
Proofreader: Safis Editing
Indexer: Mariammal Chettiyar
Graphics: Jason Monteiro
Production Coordinator: Shantanu Zagade

First published: August 2018

Production reference: 1300818

Published by Packt Publishing Ltd.
Livery Place
35 Livery Street
Birmingham
B3 2PB, UK.

ISBN 978-1-78847-950-9

www.packtpub.com

`mapt.io`

Mapt is an online digital library that gives you full access to over 5,000 books and videos, as well as industry leading tools to help you plan your personal development and advance your career. For more information, please visit our website.

Why subscribe?

- Spend less time learning and more time coding with practical eBooks and Videos from over 4,000 industry professionals

- Improve your learning with Skill Plans built especially for you

- Get a free eBook or video every month

- Mapt is fully searchable

- Copy and paste, print, and bookmark content

PacktPub.com

Did you know that Packt offers eBook versions of every book published, with PDF and ePub files available? You can upgrade to the eBook version at `www.PacktPub.com` and as a print book customer, you are entitled to a discount on the eBook copy. Get in touch with us at `service@packtpub.com` for more details.

At `www.PacktPub.com`, you can also read a collection of free technical articles, sign up for a range of free newsletters, and receive exclusive discounts and offers on Packt books and eBooks.

Contributors

About the author

Paul Osman has been building external and internal platforms for over 10 years. From public APIs targeted at third parties to internal platform teams, he has helped build distributed systems that power large-scale consumer applications. He has managed teams of engineers to rapidly deliver service-based software systems with confidence.

Paul has published articles and given multiple conference talks on microservices and DevOps. He is a passionate advocate of open technology platforms and tools.

Packt is searching for authors like you

If you're interested in becoming an author for Packt, please visit `authors.packtpub.com` and apply today. We have worked with thousands of developers and tech professionals, just like you, to help them share their insight with the global tech community. You can make a general application, apply for a specific hot topic that we are recruiting an author for, or submit your own idea.

Table of Contents

Preface

Why microservices?

Microservices has become an increasingly popular subject over the last few years. As with any new architectural concept, there is plenty of room for misunderstanding. Even the term microservices is confusing. Newcomers are often unsure about the appropriate size of a microservice (hint: it's not actually about the size of the code base) and can get stuck on how to get started with this architectural style.

Service-oriented architectures are nothing new. Web services were being promoted by various companies in the 1990s as a solution to large, inflexible code bases. The promise was that web services would provide reusable capabilities that could be easily consumed by your code bases. Technologies such as SOAP and WSDL started gaining adoption, but never seemed to deliver on the ease of use promise. Meanwhile, open source languages such as PHP, Ruby, and Python with frameworks such as Symfony, Rails, and Django made developing monolithic web-centric code bases easier.

Fast forward a couple of decades and we started seeing a renewed interest in services. So, what's changed? For one, with the advent of rich web and mobile applications, every system is now a distributed system. Thanks to the advent of cloud computing, compute and storage resources are cheaper than they've ever been. Containers are changing the way we think about deploying and operating our services. Many consumer services are outgrowing their monolithic code bases, and teams are finding them hard to scale. Microservices can help with many of these challenges.

Microservice prerequisites

Microservices aren't a panacea. While they have many benefits (which we'll discuss later), they also introduce some specific challenges. Before deciding to make the move to microservices, it's important to have certain infrastructure and tooling in place. Martin Fowler has written about Microservices Prerequisites (https://martinfowler.com/bliki/MicroservicePrerequisites.html), as has Phil Calcado (http://philcalcado.com/2017/06/11/calcados_microservices_prerequisites.html). I won't repeat what others have written; instead, I will just say that it pays to have a certain amount of automation and monitoring in place before you start developing microservices. Your teams should be comfortable sharing on-call duties and you should have a system for managing alerts and escalations, such as PagerDuty (http://pagerduty.com/).

Microservices benefits

The various benefits of microservices are as discussed in the next sections.

Scaling

In a monolithic code base, scaling is an all-or-nothing approach. Microservices make it easier to scale separate parts of your application based on their own needs. For example, you might have a particular part of your application that is in the critical path of every user request (that is, authentication/authorization services), whereas other parts are only used by a subset of your users (that is, search or messaging). Different traffic patterns will translate to different scaling needs and different techniques that should be used to scale a service. A service that requires a read for every request from a user should use a data store that makes reads cheap. Services that do not need to provide strongly consistent results can take advantage of extensive caching.

Team organization

When teams of engineers are working on separate code bases with separate deployments, they are able to make a lot of decisions independently, without the need to coordinate with other teams in the organization. This means that engineers are free to commit code, design their own code review processes, and deploy to production without always needing to coordinate. In a monolith, it's not uncommon for engineers to have to get their changes into a queue that is then deployed at a set time with changes from other teams. If something goes wrong (poison deploys are one of the most common causes of outages), then the whole change set gets rolled back, delaying work by multiple teams. Microservices help you avoid this by allowing teams to move with more autonomy.

Reliability

When a monolith fails, it tends to fail completely. A database is unavailable, and then the application tries to use stale connections in a connection pool, eventually the threads or processes serving requests lock up, and users are left with a white screen of death or a inoperable mobile application. Microservices allow you to decide on a case-by-case basis how a failure in a particular part of your application should be treated. If your service cannot reach a database, perhaps it's better to return a stale cache, or an empty response. If your service has to throw up its hands and start returning HTTP 503 responses, upstream services can respond by applying back pressure, allowing the service to catch up. Microservices give you much more freedom to isolate failures in your system, resulting in a happier experience for your users.

This book will serve as a handy reference for many of the subjects that will come up as you develop microservices. We'll start with recipes that will help you make the transition from a monolith to a suite of microservices. Subsequent chapters will address specific areas or challenges that come up when choosing how best to architect and manage your microservices. Recipes that cover code will include working, simple, tested examples that you can use in your own applications. My hope is that this book will help you think about, plan, and execute the development of microservice-based applications. Enjoy!

Who this book is for

If you are a developer who would like to build effective and scalable microservices, then this book is for you. Basic knowledge of the microservices architecture is assumed.

What this book covers

Chapter 1, *Breaking the Monolith*, shows how to make the transition from monolith to microservices, with the recipes focused on architectural design. You'll learn how to manage some of the initial challenges when you begin to develop features using this new architectural style.

Chapter 2, *Edge Services*, teaches you how to use open source software to expose your services to the public internet, control routing, extend your service's functionality, and handle a number of common challenges when deploying and scaling microservices.

`Chapter 3`, *Inter-Service Communication*, discusses recipes that will enable you to confidently handle the various kinds of interactions we're bound to require in a microservice architecture.

`Chapter 4`, *Client Patterns*, discusses techniques for modeling dependent service calls and aggregating responses from various services to create client-specific APIs. We'll also discuss managing different microservices environments and making RPC consistent with JSON and HTTP, as well as the gRPC and Thrift binary protocols.

`Chapter 5`, *Reliability Patterns*, discusses a number of useful reliability patterns that can be used when designing and building microservices to prepare for and reduce the impact of system failures, both expected and unexpected.

`Chapter 6`, *Security*, includes recipes that will help you learn a number of good practices to consider when building, deploying, and operating microservices.

`Chapter 7`, *Monitoring and Observability*, introduces several tenants of monitoring and observability. We'll demonstrate how to modify our services to emit structured logs. We'll also take a look at metrics, using a number of different systems for collecting, aggregating, and visualizing metrics.

`Chapter 8`, *Scaling*, discusses load testing using different tools. We will also set up auto-scaling groups in AWS, making them scalable on demand. This will be followed by strategies for capacity planning.

`Chapter 9`, *Deploying Microservices*, discusses containers, orchestration, and scheduling, and various methods for safely shipping changes to users. The recipes in this chapter should serve as a good starting point, especially if you're accustomed to deploying monoliths on virtual machines or bare metal servers.

To get the most out of this book

This books assumes basic knowledge of microservices architectures. Other instructions are mentioned in the respective recipes as needed.

Download the example code files

You can download the example code files for this book from your account at `www.packtpub.com`. If you purchased this book elsewhere, you can visit `www.packtpub.com/support` and register to have the files emailed directly to you.

You can download the code files by following these steps:

1. Log in or register at www.packtpub.com.
2. Select the **SUPPORT** tab.
3. Click on **Code Downloads & Errata**.
4. Enter the name of the book in the **Search** box and follow the onscreen instructions.

Once the file is downloaded, please make sure that you unzip or extract the folder using the latest version of:

- WinRAR/7-Zip for Windows
- Zipeg/iZip/UnRarX for Mac
- 7-Zip/PeaZip for Linux

The code bundle for the book is also hosted on GitHub at https://github.com/ PacktPublishing/Microservices-Development-Cookbook. We also have other code bundles from our rich catalog of books and videos available at https://github.com/ PacktPublishing/. Check them out!

Conventions used

There are a number of text conventions used throughout this book.

CodeInText: Indicates code words in text, database table names, folder names, filenames, file extensions, pathnames, dummy URLs, user input, and Twitter handles. Here is an example: "Open the newly created service object in the app/services/attachments_service.rb file and move the responsibility for uploading the file to the AttachmentsService#upload method."

A block of code is set as follows:

```
class AttachmentsService

  def upload(message_id, user_id, file_name, data, media_type)
    message = Message.find_by!(message_id, user_id: user_id)
    file = StorageBucket.files.create(
      key:  file_name,
      body: StringIO.new(Base64.decode64(data), 'rb'),
      public: true
    )
```

Any command-line input or output is written as follows:

```
brew install docker-compose
```

Bold: Indicates a new term, an important word, or words that you see onscreen. For example, words in menus or dialog boxes appear in the text like this. Here is an example: "Installing and managing a Kubernetes cluster is beyond the scope of this book. Luckily, a project called **Minikube** allows you to easily run a single-node Kubernetes cluster on your development machine."

Warnings or important notes appear like this.

Tips and tricks appear like this.

Sections

In this book, you will find several headings that appear frequently (*Getting ready*, *How to do it...*).

To give clear instructions on how to complete a recipe, use these sections as follows:

Getting ready

This section tells you what to expect in the recipe and describes how to set up any software or any preliminary settings required for the recipe.

How to do it...

This section contains the steps required to follow the recipe.

Get in touch

Feedback from our readers is always welcome.

General feedback: Email `feedback@packtpub.com` and mention the book title in the subject of your message. If you have questions about any aspect of this book, please email us at `questions@packtpub.com`.

Errata: Although we have taken every care to ensure the accuracy of our content, mistakes do happen. If you have found a mistake in this book, we would be grateful if you would report this to us. Please visit `www.packtpub.com/submit-errata`, selecting your book, clicking on the Errata Submission Form link, and entering the details.

Piracy: If you come across any illegal copies of our works in any form on the internet, we would be grateful if you would provide us with the location address or website name. Please contact us at `copyright@packtpub.com` with a link to the material.

If you are interested in becoming an author: If there is a topic that you have expertise in and you are interested in either writing or contributing to a book, please visit `authors.packtpub.com`.

Reviews

Please leave a review. Once you have read and used this book, why not leave a review on the site that you purchased it from? Potential readers can then see and use your unbiased opinion to make purchase decisions, we at Packt can understand what you think about our products, and our authors can see your feedback on their book. Thank you!

For more information about Packt, please visit `packtpub.com`.

Breaking the Monolith

1

In this chapter, we will cover the following recipes:

- Organizing your team to embrace microservices
- Decomposing by business capability
- Identifying bounded contexts
- Migrating data in production
- Refactoring your monolith
- Evolving your monolith into services
- Evolving your test suite
- Using Docker for local development
- Routing requests to services

Introduction

One of the hardest things about microservices is getting started. Many teams have found themselves building features into an ever-growing, hard-to-manage monolithic code base and don't know how to start breaking it apart into more manageable, separately deployable services. The recipes in this chapter will explain how to make the transition from monolith to microservices. Many of the recipes will involve no code whatsoever; instead, they will be focused on architectural design and how best to structure teams to work on microservices.

You'll learn how to begin moving from a single monolithic code base to suites of microservices. You'll also learn how to manage some of the initial challenges when you begin to develop features using this new architectural style.

Organizing your team

Conway's law tells us that organizations will produce designs whose structure is a copy of their communication structure. This often means that the organizational chart of an engineering team will have a profound impact on the structure of the designs of the software it produces. When a new startup begins building software, the team is small—sometimes it is comprised of just one or two engineers. In this setup, engineers work on everything, including frontend and backend systems, as well as operations. Monoliths suit this organizational structure very well, allowing engineers to work on any part of the system at any given time without moving between code bases.

As a team grows, and you start to consider the benefits of microservices, you can consider employing a technique commonly referred to as an the **Inverse Conway Maneuver**. This technique recommends evolving your team and organizational structure to encourage the kind of architectural style you want to see emerge. With regard to microservices, this will usually involve organizing engineers into small teams that you will eventually want to be responsible for a handful of related services. Setting your team up for this structure ahead of time can motivate engineers to build services by limiting communication and decision-making overhead within the team. Simply put, monoliths continue to exist when the cost of adding features as services is greater than the cost of adding a feature to the monolith. Organizing your teams in this way reduces the cost of developing services.

This recipe is aimed at managers and other leaders in companies who have the influence to implement changes to the structure of the organization.

How to do it...

Re-organizing a team is never a simple task, and there are many non-obvious factors to consider. Factors such as personality, individual strengths and weaknesses, and past histories are outside the scope of this recipe, but they should be considered carefully when making any changes. The steps in this recipe provide one possible way to move a team from being organized around a monolithic code base to being optimized for microservices, but there is no one-size-fits-all recipe for every organization.

Use the following steps as a guide if you think they apply, but otherwise use them for inspiration and to encourage thought and discussion:

1. Working with other stakeholders in your organization, build out a product roadmap. You may have limited information about the challenges your organization will face in the short term, but do the best you can. It's perfectly natural to be very detailed for short-term items on a roadmap and very general for the longer term.

2. Using the product roadmap, try to identify technical capabilities that will be required to help you deliver value to your users. For example, you may be planning to work on a feature that relies heavily on search. You may also have a number of features that rely on content uploading and management. This means that search and uploading are two technical capabilities you know you will need to invest in.

3. As you see patterns emerge, try to identify the main functional areas of your application, paying attention to how much work you anticipate will go into each area. Assign higher priorities to the functional areas you anticipate will need a lot of investment in the short to medium term.

4. Create new teams, ideally consisting of four to six engineers, who are responsible for one of the functional areas within your application. Start with the functional areas that you anticipate will require the most work over the next quarter or so. These teams can be focused on the backend services or they can be cross-functional teams that include the mobile and web engineers. The benefit of having cross-functional teams is that the team can then deliver the entire vertical component of the application autonomously. The combination of service engineers with engineers consuming their services will also enable more information sharing, and hopefully, empathy.

Discussion

Using this approach, you should end up with small, cohesive, and focused teams responsible for core areas of your application. The nature of teams is that individuals within the team should start to see the benefit of creating separately managed and deployed code bases that they can work in autonomously without the costly overhead of coordinating changes and deployments with other teams.

To help illustrate these steps, imagine your organization builds an image-messaging application. The application allows users to take a photo with their smart phone and send it, along with a message, to a friend in their contacts list. Their friends can also send them photos with messages. A fictional roadmap for this fictional product could involve the need to add support for short videos, photo filters, and support for emojis. You now know that the ability to record, upload, and play videos, the ability to apply photo filters, and the ability to send rich text will be important to your organization. Additionally, you know from experience that users need to register, log in, and maintain a friends list.

Using the preceding example, you may decide to organize engineers into a media team, responsible for uploading, processing and playing, filters, and storage and delivery, a messaging team, responsible for the sending of photo or video messages with associated text, and a users team, responsible for providing reliable authentication, registration, on-boarding, and social features.

Decomposing by business capability

In the early stages of product development, monoliths are the best suited to delivering features to users as quickly and simply as possible. This is appropriate, as at this point in a products development you do not have luxury problems of having to scale your teams, code bases or ability to serve customer traffic. Following good design practices, you separate your applications concerns into easy-to-read, modular code patterns. Doing so allows engineers to work on different sections of the code autonomously and limits the possibility of having to untangle complicated merge conflicts when it comes time to merge your branch into the master and deploy your code.

Microservices require you to go a step further than the good design practices you've already been following in your monolith. To organize your small, autonomous teams around microservices, you should consider first identifying the core business capabilities that your application provides. Business capability is a business school term that describes the various ways your organization produces value. For example, your internal order management is responsible for processing customer orders. If you have a social application that allows users to submit user-generated content such as photos, your photo upload system provides a business capability.

When thinking about system design, business capabilities are closely related to the **Single Responsibility Principle (SRP)** from **object-oriented design (OOD)**. Microservices are essentially SRP extended to code bases. Thinking about this will help you design appropriately sized microservices. Services should have one primary job and they should do it well. This could be storing and serving images, delivering messages, or creating and authenticating user accounts.

How to do it...

Decomposing your monolith by business capability is a process. These steps can be carried out in parallel for each new service you identify a need for, but you may want to start with one service and apply the lessons you learn to subsequent efforts:

1. Identify a business capability that is currently provided by your monolith. This will be the target for our first service. Ideally this business capability is something that has some focus on the roadmap you worked on in the previous recipe and ownership can be given to one of your newly created teams. Let's use our fictional photo messaging service as an example and assume we'll start with the ability to upload and display media as our first identified business capability. This functionality is currently implemented as a single model and controller in your **Ruby on Rails** monolith:

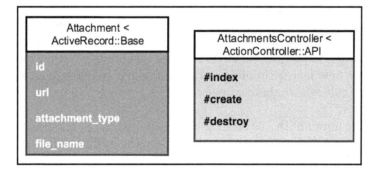

2. In the preceding screenshot, **AttachmentsController** has four methods (called **actions** in Ruby on Rails lingo), which roughly correspond to the **create, retrieve, update, delete** (**CRUD**) operations you want to perform on an **Attachment** resource. We don't strictly need it, and so will omit the update action. This maps very nicely to a RESTful service, so you can design, implement, and deploy a microservice with the following API:

```
POST /attachments
GET /attachments/:id
DELETE /attachments/:id
```

3. With the new microservice deployed (migrating data is discussed in a later recipe), you can now begin modifying client code paths to use the new service. You can begin by replacing the code in the **AttachmentsController** action's methods to make an HTTP request to our new microservice. Techniques for doing this are covered in the *Evolving your monolith into services* recipe later in this chapter.

Identifying bounded contexts

When designing microservices, a common point of confusion is how big or small a service should be. This confusion can lead engineers to focus on things such as the number of lines of code in a particular service. Lines of code are an awful metric for measuring software; it's much more useful to focus on the role that a service plays, both in terms of the business capability it provides and the domain objects it helps manage. We want to design services that have low coupling with other services, because this limits what we have to change when introducing a new feature in our product or making changes to an existing one. We also want to give services a single responsibility.

When decomposing a monolith, it's often useful to look at the data model when deciding what services to extract. In our fictional image-messaging application, we can imagine the following data model:

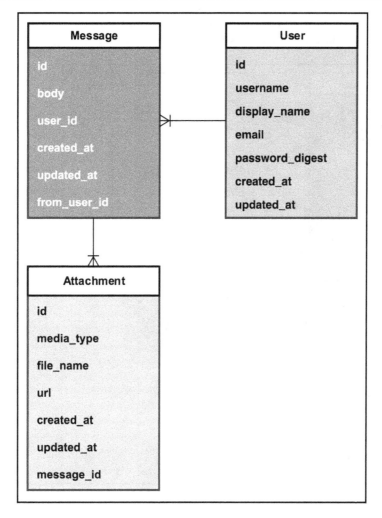

We have a table for messages, a table for users, and a table for attachments. The **Message** entity has a one-to-many relationship with the **User** entity; every user can have many messages that originate from or are targeted at them, and every message can have multiple attachments. What happens as the application evolves and we add more features? The preceding data model does not include anything about social graphs. Let's imagine that we want a user to be able to follow other users. We'll define the following as a asymmetric relationship, just because user 1 follows user 2, that does not mean that user 2 follows user 1.

There are a number of ways to model this kind of relationship; we'll focus on one of the simplest, which is an adjacency list. Take a look at the following diagram:

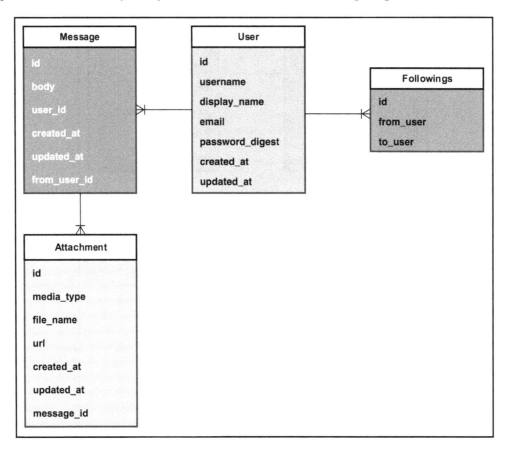

We now have an entity, **Followings**, to represent a follow relationship between two users. This works perfectly in our monolith, but introduces a challenge with microservices. If we were to build two new services, one to handle attachments, and another to handle the social graph (two distinct responsibilities), we now have two definitions of the user. This duplication of models is often necessary. The alternative is to have multiple services access and make updates to the same model, which is extremely brittle and can quickly lead to unreliable code.

This is where bounded contexts can help. A bounded context is a term from **Domain-Driven Design** (**DDD**) and it defines the area of a system within which a particular model makes sense. In the preceding example, the social-graph service would have a **User** model whose bounded context would be the users social graph (easy enough). The media service would have a **User** model whose bounded context would be photos and videos. Identifying these bounded contexts is important, especially when deconstructing a monolith—you'll often find that as a monolithic code base grows, the previously discussed business capabilities (uploading and viewing photos and videos, and user relationships) would probably end up sharing the same, bloated **User** model, which will then have to be untangled. This can be a tricky but enlightening and important process.

How to do it...

Deciding on how to define bounded contexts within a system can be a rewarding endeavor. The process itself encourages teams to have many interesting discussions about the models in a system and the various interactions that must happen between various systems:

1. Before a team can start to define the bounded contexts it works with, it should first start listing the models that are owned by the parts of the system it works on. For example, the media team will obviously own the **Attachment** model, but it will also need to have information about users, and messages. The **Attachment** model may be entirely maintained within the context of the media teams services, but the others will have to have a well-defined bounded context that can be communicated to other teams if necessary.

2. Once a team has identified potentially shared models, it's a good idea to have a discussion with other teams that use similar models or the same model.

3. In those discussions, hammer out the boundaries of the model and decide whether it makes sense to share a model implementation (which in a microservice world would necessitate a service-to-service call) or go their separate ways and develop and maintain separate model implementations. If the choice is made to develop separate model implementations, it'll become important to clearly define the bounded context within which the model applies.

4. The team should document clear boundaries in terms of teams, specific parts of the application, or specific code bases that should make use of the model.

Migrating data in production

Monolith code bases usually use a primary relational database for persistence. Modern web frameworks are often packaged with **object-relational mapping** (**ORM**), which allows you to define your domain objects using classes that correspond to tables in the database. Instances of these model classes correspond to rows in the table. As monolith code bases grow, it's not uncommon to see additional data stores, such as document or key value stores, be added.

Microservices should not share access with the same database your monolith connects to. Doing so will inevitably cause problems when trying to coordinate data migrations, such as schema changes. Even schema-less stores will cause problems when you change the way data is written in one code base but not how data is read in another code base. For this and other reasons, it's best to have microservices fully manage the data stores they use for persistence.

When transitioning from a monolith to microservices, it's important to have a strategy for how to migrate data. All too often, a team will extract the code for a microservice and leave the data, setting themselves up for future pain. In addition to difficulty managing migrations, a failure in the monolith relational database will now have cascading impacts on services, leading to difficult-to-debug production incidents.

One popular technique for managing large-scale data migrations is to set up dual writing. When your new service is deployed, you'll have two write paths–one from the original monolith code base to its database and one from your new service to its own data store. Make sure that writes go to both of these code paths. You'll now be replicating data from the moment your new service goes into production, allowing you to backfill older data using a script or a similar offline task. Once data is being written to both data stores, you can now modify all of your various read paths. Wherever the code is used to query the monolith database directly, replace the query with a call to your new service. Once all read paths have been modified, remove any write paths that are still writing to the old location. Now you can delete the old data (you have backups, right?).

How to do it...

Migrating data from a monolith database to a new store fronted by a new service, without any impact on availability or consistency, is a difficult but common task when making the transition to microservices. Using our fictional photo-messaging application, we can imagine a scenario where we want to create a new microservice responsible for handling media uploads. In this scenario, we'd follow a common dual-writing pattern:

1. Before writing a new service to handle media uploads, we'll assume that the monolith architecture looks something like the following diagram, where HTTP requests are being handled by the monolith, which presumably reads the multipart/form-encoded content body as a binary object and stores the file in a distributed file store (Amazon's S3 service, for example). Metadata about the file is then written to a database table, called **attachments**, as shown in the following diagram:

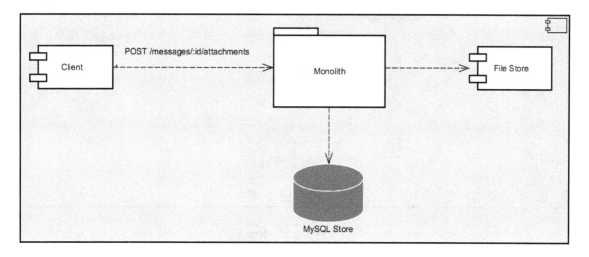

2. After writing a new service, you now have two write paths. In the write path in the monolith, make a call to your service so that you're replicating the data in the monolith database as well as the database fronted by your new service. You're now duplicating new data and can write a script to backfill older data. Your architecture now looks something like this:

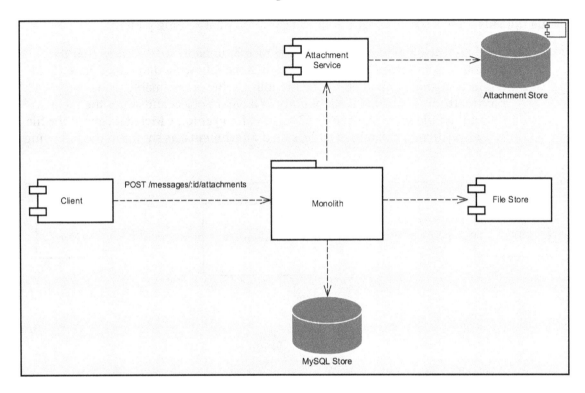

3. Find all read paths in your **Client** and **Monolith** code, and update them to use your new service. All reads will now be going to your service, which will be able to give consistent results.
4. Find all write paths in your **Client** and **Monolith** code, and update them to use your new service. All reads and writes are now going to your service, and you can safely delete old data and code paths. Your final architecture should look something like the following (we'll discuss edge proxies in later chapters):

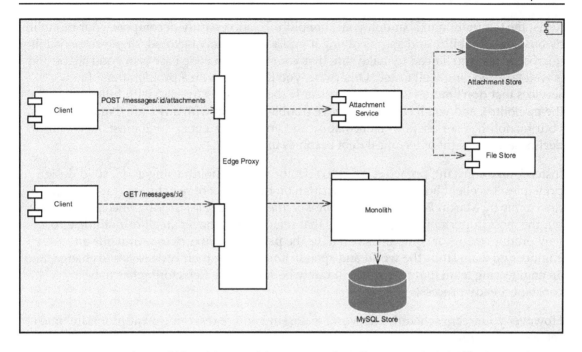

Using this approach, you'll be able to safely migrate data from a monolith database to a new store created for a new microservice without the need for downtime. It's important not to skip this step; otherwise, you won't truly realize the benefits of microservice architectures (although, arguably, you'll experience all the downsides!).

Refactoring your monolith

A common mistake when making the transition to microservices is to ignore the monolith and just build new features as services. This usually happens when a team feels that the monolith has gotten so out of control, and the code so unwieldy, that it would be better to declare bankruptcy and leave it to rot. This can be especially tempting because the idea of building green field code with no legacy baggage sounds a lot nicer than refactoring brittle, legacy code.

Resist the temptation to abandon your monolith. To successfully decompose your monolith by business capability and start evolving it into a set of nicely factored, single-responsibility microservices, you'll need to make sure that your monolith code base is in good shape and is well factored, and well tested. Otherwise, you'll end up with a proliferation of new services that don't model your domain cleanly (because they overlap with functionality in the monolith), and you'll continue to have trouble working with any code that exists in your monolith. Your users won't be happy and your teams' energy will most likely start to decline as the weight of technical debt becomes unbearable.

Instead, take constant, proactive steps to refactor your monolith using good, solid design principles. Excellent books have been written on the subject of refactoring (I recommend *Refactoring* by Martin Fowler and *Working Effectively with Legacy Code* by Michael Feathers), but the most important thing to know is that refactoring is never an all-or-nothing effort. Few product teams or companies will have the patience or luxury to wait while an engineering team stops the world and spends time making their code easier to change, and an engineering team that tries this will rarely be successful. Refactoring has to be a constant, steady process.

However your team schedules its work, make sure you're reserving an appropriate time for refactoring. A guiding principle is, whenever you go to make a change, first make the change easy to make, then make the change. Your goal is to make your monolith code easier to work with, easier to understand, and less brittle. You should also be able to develop a robust test suite that will come in handy.

Once your monolith is in better shape, you can start to continuously shrink the monolith as you factor out services. Another aspect of most monolith code bases is serving dynamically generated views and static assets served through browsers. If your monolith is responsible for this, consider moving your web application component into a separately served JavaScript application. This will allow you to shrink your monolith from multiple directions.

How to do it...

Refactoring any code base is a process. For monoliths, there are a few techniques that can work quite well. In this example, we'll document the steps that can be taken to make refactoring a Ruby on Rails code base easy:

1. Using the techniques described in previous recipes, identify business capabilities and bounded contexts within your application. Let's focus on the ability to upload pictures and videos.

2. Create a directory called `app/services` alongside `controllers`, `models`, and `views`. This directory will hold all of your service objects. Service objects are a pattern used in many Rails applications to factor out a conceptual service into a ruby object that does not inherit any Ruby on Rails functionality. This will make it easier to move the functionality encapsulated within a service object into a separate microservice. There is no one way to structure your service objects. I prefer to have each object represent a service, and move operations I want that service to be responsible for to that service object as methods.

3. Create a new file called `attachments_service.rb` under `app/services` and give it the following definition:

```ruby
class AttachmentsService

  def upload
    # ...
  end

  def delete!
    # ...
  end

end
```

4. Looking at the source code for the `AttachmentsController#create` method in the `app/controllers/attachments_controller.rb` file, it currently handles the responsibility for creating the `Attachment` instance and uploading the file data to the attachment store, which in this case is an Amazon S3 bucket. This is the functionality that we need to move to the newly created service object:

```ruby
# POST /messages/:message_id/attachments
def create
  message = Message.find_by!(params[:message_id], user_id:
  current_user.id)
  file = StorageBucket.files.create(
    key:  params[:file][:name],
    body: StringIO.new(Base64.decode64(params[:file][:data]),
    'rb'),
    public: true
  )
  attachment = Attachment.new(attachment_params.merge!(message:
  message))
  attachment.url = file.public_url
  attachment.file_name = params[:file][:name]
```

```
    attachment.save
    json_response({ url: attachment.url }, :created)
end
```

5. Open the newly created service object in
   the `app/services/attachments_service.rb` file and move the responsibility
   for uploading the file to the `AttachmentsService#upload` method:

```
class AttachmentsService

  def upload(message_id, user_id, file_name, data, media_type)
    message = Message.find_by!(message_id, user_id: user_id)
    file = StorageBucket.files.create(
      key:  file_name,
      body: StringIO.new(Base64.decode64(data), 'rb'),
      public: true
    )
    Attachment.create(
      media_type: media_type,
      file_name:  file_name,
      url:        file.public_url,
      message:    message
    )
  end

  def delete!
  end
end
```

6. Now upload the `AttachmentsController#create` method in
   `app/controllers/attachments_controller.rb` to use the newly created
   `AttachmentsService#upload` method:

```
# POST /messages/:message_id/attachments
def create
  service = AttachmentService.new
  attachment = service.upload(params[:message_id], current_user.id,
    params[:file][:name], params[:file][:data],
    params[:media_type])
  json_response({ url: attachment.url }, :created)
end
```

7. Repeat this process for code in the `AttachmentsController#destroy` method, moving the responsibility to the new service object. When you're finished, no code in `AttachmentsController` should be interacting with the `Attachments` model directly; instead, it should be going through the `AttachmentsService` service object.

You've now isolated responsibility for the management of attachments to a single service class. This class should encapsulate all of the business logic that will eventually be moved to a new attachment service.

Evolving your monolith into services

One of the most complicated aspects of transitioning from a monolith to services can be request routing. In later recipes and chapters, we'll explore the topic of exposing your services to the internet so that the mobile and web client applications can communicate directly with them. For now, however, having your monolith act as a router can serve as a useful intermediary step.

As you break your monolith into small, maintainable microservices, you can replace code paths in your monolith with calls to your services. Depending on the programming language or framework you used to build your monolith, these sections of code can be called controller actions, views, or something else. We'll continue to assume that your monolith was built in the popular Ruby on Rails framework; in which case, we'll be looking at controller actions. We'll also assume that you've begun refactoring your monolith and have created one or more service objects as described in the previous recipe.

It's important when doing this to follow best practices. In later chapters, we'll introduce concepts, such as circuit breakers, that become important when doing service-to-service communication. For now, be mindful that HTTP calls from your monolith to a service could fail, and you should consider how best to handle that kind of situation.

How to do it...

1. Open the service object we created in the previous recipe. We'll modify the service object to be able to call an external microservice responsible for managing attachments. For the sake of simplicity, we'll use an HTTP client that is provided in the Ruby standard library. The service object should be in the `app/services/attachments_service.rb` file:

```
class AttachmentsService

  BASE_URI = "http://attachment-service.yourorg.example.com/"

  def upload(message_id, user_id, file_name, data, media_type)
    body = {
      user_id: user_id,
      file_name: file_name,
      data: StringIO.new(Base64.decode64(params[:file]
      [:data]), 'rb'),
      message: message_id,
      media_type: media_type
    }.to_json
    uri = URI("#{BASE_URI}attachment")
    headers = { "Content-Type" => "application/json" }
    Net::HTTP.post(uri, body, headers)
  end

end
```

2. Open the `attachments_controller.rb` file, located in `pichat/app/controllers/`, and look at the following create action. Because of the refactoring work done in the previous chapter, we require only a small change to make the controller work with our new service object:

```
class AttachmentsController < ApplicationController
  # POST /messages/:message_id/attachments
  def create
    service = AttachmentService.new
    response = service.upload(params[:message_id], current_user.id,
     params[:file][:name], params[:file][:data],
     params[:media_type])
    json_response(response.body, response.code)
  end
  # ...
end
```

Evolving your test suite

Having a good test suite in the first place will help tremendously as you move from a monolith to microservices. Each time you remove functionality from your monolith code base, your tests will need to be updated. It's tempting to replace unit and functional tests in your Rails app with tests that make external network calls to your services, but this approach has a number of downsides. Tests that make external calls will be prone to failures caused by intermittent network connectivity issues and will take an enormous amount of time to run after a while.

Instead of making external network calls, you should modify your monolith tests to stub microservices. Tests that use stubs to represent calls to microservices will be less brittle and will run faster. As long as your microservices satisfy the API contracts you develop, the tests will be reliable indicators of your monolith code base's health. Making backwards-incompatible changes to your microservices is another topic that will be covered in a later recipe.

Getting ready

We'll use the `webmock` gem for stubbing out external HTTP requests in our tests, so update your monolith gemfile to include the `webmock` gem in the test group:

```
group :test do
  # ...
  gem 'webmock'
end
```

You should also update `spec/spec_helper.rb` to disable external network requests. That will keep you honest when writing the rest of your test code:

```
require 'webmock/rspec'
WebMock.disable_net_connect!(allow_localhost: false)
```

How to do it...

Now that you have `webmock` included in your project, you can start stubbing HTTP requests in your specs. Once again, open `specs/spec_helper.rb` and add the following content:

```
stub_request(:post, "attachment-service.yourorg.example.com").
  with(body: {media_type: 1}, headers: {"Content-Type" => /image\/.+/}).
  to_return(body: { foo: bar })
```

Using Docker for local development

As we've discussed, microservices solve a particular set of problems but introduce some new challenges of their own. One challenge that engineers on your team will probably run into is doing local development. With a monolith, there are fewer moving parts that have to be managed—usually, you can get away with just running a database and an application server on your workstation to get work done. As you start to create new microservices, however, the situation gets more complicated.

Containers are a great way to manage this complexity. Docker is a popular, open source software containerization platform. Docker allows you to specify how to run your application as a container—a lightweight standardized unit for deployment. There are plenty of books and online documentation about Docker, so we won't go into too much detail here, just know that a container encapsulates all of the information needed to run your application. As mentioned, a monolith application will often require an application server and a database server at a minimum—these will each run in their own container.

Docker Compose is a tool for running multicontainer applications. Compose allows you to define your applications containers in a YAML configuration file. Using the information in this file, you can then build and run your application. Compose will manage all of the various services defined in the configuration file in separate containers, allowing you to run a complex system on your workstation for local development.

Getting ready

Before you can follow the steps in this recipe, you'll need to install the required software:

1. Install Docker. Download the installation package from the Docker website (`https://www.docker.com/docker-mac`) and follow the instructions.

2. Install `docker-compose` by executing the following command line on macOS X:

```
brew install docker-compose
```

   On Ubuntu Linux, you can execute the following command line:

```
apt-get install docker-compose
```

With those two packages installed, you'll be ready to follow the steps in this recipe.

How to do it...

1. In the root directory of your Rails application, create a single file called `Dockerfile` with the following contents:

```
FROM ruby:2.3.3
RUN apt-get update -qq && apt-get install -y build-essential
libpq-dev nodejs
RUN mkdir /pichat
WORKDIR /pichat
ADD Gemfile /pichat/Gemfile
ADD Gemfile.lock /pichat/Gemfile.lock
RUN bundle install
ADD . /pichat
```

2. Create a file called `docker-compose.yml` with the following contents:

```
version: '3'
services:
  db:
    image: mysql:5.6.34
    ports:
      - "3306:3306"
    environment:
      MYSQL_ROOT_PASSWORD: root

  app:
    build: .
    environment:
```

```
    RAILS_ENV: development
  command: bundle exec rails s -p 3000 -b '0.0.0.0'
  volumes:
    - .:/pichat
  ports:
    - "3000:3000"
  depends_on:
    - db
```

3. Start your application by running the `docker-compose up app` command. You should be able to access your monolith by entering `http://localhost:3000/` in your browser. You can use this approach for new services that you write.

Routing requests to services

In previous recipes, we focused on having your monolith route requests to services. This technique is a good start since it requires no client changes to work. Your clients still make requests to your monolith and your monolith marshals the request to your microservices through its controller actions. At some point, however, to truly benefit from a microservices architecture, you'll want to remove the monolith from the critical path and allow your clients to make requests to your microservices. It's not uncommon for an engineer to expose their organization's first microservice to the internet directly, usually using a different hostname. However, this starts to become unmanageable as you develop more services and need a certain amount of consistency when it comes to monitoring, security, and reliability concerns.

Internet-facing systems face a number of challenges. They need to be able to handle a number of security concerns, rate limiting, periodic spikes in traffic, and so on. Doing this for each service you expose to the public internet will become very expensive, very quickly. Instead, you should consider having a single edge service that supports routing requests from the public internet to internal services. A good edge service should support common features, such as dynamic path rewriting, load shedding, and authentication. Luckily, there are a number of good open source edge service solutions. In this recipe, we'll use a Netflix project called **Zuul**.

How to do it...

1. Create a new Spring Boot service called `Edge Proxy` with a main class called `EdgeProxyApplication`.

2. Spring Cloud includes an embedded Zuul proxy. Enable it by adding the `@EnableZuulProxy` annotation to your `EdgeProxyApplication` class:

```
package com.packtpub.microservices;

import org.springframework.boot.SpringApplication;
import
org.springframework.boot.autoconfigure.SpringBootApplication;
import org.springframework.cloud.netflix.zuul.EnableZuulProxy;

@EnableZuulProxy
@SpringBootApplication
public class EdgeProxyApplication {

  public static void main(String[] args) {
    SpringApplication.run(EdgeProxyApplication.class, args);
  }

}
```

3. Create a file called `application.properties` under `src/main/resources/` with the following contents:

```
zuul.routes.media.url=http://localhost:8090
ribbon.eureka.enabled=false
server.port=8080
```

In the preceding code, it tells `zuul` to route requests to `/media` to a service running on port `8090`. We'll touch on that `eureka` option in later chapters when we discuss service discovery, for now just make sure it's set to `false`.

At this point, your service should be able to proxy requests to the appropriate service. You've just taken one of the biggest steps toward building a microservices architecture. Congratulations!

Edge Services 2

In this chapter, we will cover the following recipes:

- Controlling access to your service with an edge proxy server
- Extending your services with sidecars
- Using API Gateway to route requests to services
- Rate limiting with an edge proxy server
- Stopping cascading failure with Hystrix
- Using a service mesh to factor out shared concerns

Introduction

Now that you've had some experience breaking a monolith into microservices, you've seen that many of the challenges exist outside the monolith or service code bases themselves. Exposing your service to the internet, controlling routing, and building in resiliency are all concerns that can be addressed by what are commonly called **edge services**. These are services that exist at the edge of our architecture, generally handling requests from the public internet. Luckily, because many of these challenges are so common, open source projects exist to handle most of them for us. We'll use a lot of great open source software in this chapter.

With the recipes in this chapter, you'll learn how to use open source software to expose your services to the public internet, control routing, extend your service's functionality, and handle a number of common challenges when deploying and scaling microservices. You'll also learn about techniques for making client development against services easier and how to standardize the monitoring and observability of your microservice architecture.

Controlling access to your service with an edge proxy server

In `Chapter 1`, *Breaking the Monolith*, we modified a monolith code base to provide easy routing to our microservices. This approach works and requires little effort, making it an ideal intermediary step. Eventually, your monolith will become a bottleneck in the development and resiliency of your architecture. As you try to scale your service and build more microservices, your monolith will need to be updated and deployed every time you make an API change to your service. Additionally, your monolith will have to handle connections to your services and is probably not well-configured to handle edge concerns such as load shedding or circuit breaking. In the *Routing requests to services* recipe of `Chapter 1`, *Breaking the Monolith*, we introduced the concept of edge proxies. Using an edge proxy server to expose your service to the public internet allows you to factor out most of the shared concerns a publicly exposed service must address. Requirements such as request routing, load shedding, back pressure, and authentication can all be handled in a single edge proxy layer instead of being duplicated by every service you need to have exposed to the internet.

An edge proxy is a proxy server that sits on the edge of your infrastructure, providing access to internal services. You can think of an edge proxy as the "front door" to your internal service architecture—it allows clients on the internet to make requests to internal services you deploy. There are multiple open source edge proxies that have a robust feature set and community, so we don't have to write and maintain our own edge proxy server. One of the most popular open source edge proxy servers is called **Zuul** and is built by Netflix. Zuul is an edge service that provides dynamic routing, monitoring, resiliency, security, and more. Zuul is packaged as a Java library. Services written in the Java framework Spring Boot can use an embedded Zuul service to provide edge-proxy functionality. In this recipe, we'll walk through building a small Zuul edge proxy and configuring it to route requests to our services.

Operational notes

Continuing with our example application from the previous chapter, imagine that our photo-messaging application (we'll call it `pichat` from now on) was originally implemented as a Ruby on Rails monolithic code base. When the product first launched, we deployed the application to Amazon Web Services behind a single **Elastic Load Balancer** (**ELB**). We created a single **Auto Scale Group** (**ASG**) for the monolith, called `pichat-asg`.

Each EC2 instance in our ASG is running NGINX, which handles requests for static files (images, JavaScript, CSS) and proxies requests to unicorns running on the same host that is serving our Rails application. SSL is terminated at the ELB, and HTTP requests are forwarded to NGINX. The ELB is accessed through the DNS `monolith.pichat-int.me` name from within the **Virtual Private Cloud** (**VPC**).

We've now created a single `attachment-service`, which handles videos and images attached to messages being sent through the platform. The `attachment-service` is written in Java, using the Spring Boot platform and is deployed in its own ASG, called `attachment-service-asg`, that has its own ELB. We've created a private DNS record, called `attachment-service.pichat-int.me`, that points to this ELB.

With this architecture and topology in mind, we now want to route requests from the public internet to our Rails application or our newly created attachment service, depending on the path.

How to do it...

1. To demonstrate using Zuul to route requests to services, we'll first create a basic Java application that will serve as our edge proxy service. The Java project Spring Cloud provides an embedded Zuul service, making it pretty simple to create a service that uses the `zuul` library. We'll start by creating a basic Java application. Create the `build.gradle` file with the following content:

```
group 'com.packtpub.microservices'
version '1.0-SNAPSHOT'

buildscript {
    repositories {
        mavenCentral()
    }
    dependencies {
        classpath "org.springframework.boot:spring-boot-gradle-plugin:1.4.4.RELEASE"
        classpath "io.spring.gradle:dependency-management-plugin:0.5.6.RELEASE"
    }
}

apply plugin: 'java'
apply plugin: 'org.springframework.boot'
apply plugin: 'io.spring.dependency-management'
```

```
sourceCompatibility = 1.8

repositories {
    mavenCentral()
}

dependencyManagement {
    imports {
        mavenBom 'org.springframework.cloud:spring-cloud-
netflix:1.4.4.RELEASE'
    }
}

dependencies {
    compile group: 'org.springframework.boot', name: 'spring-boot-
starter-web', version: '1.4.4.RELEASE'
    compile group: 'org.springframework.cloud', name: 'spring-
cloud-starter-zuul'
    testCompile group: 'junit', name: 'junit', version: '4.12'
}
```

2. Create a single class called `EdgeProxyApplication`. This will serve as the entry point to our application:

```
package com.packtpub.microservices.ch02.edgeproxy;

import org.springframework.boot.SpringApplication;
import
org.springframework.boot.autoconfigure.SpringBootApplication;
import org.springframework.cloud.netflix.zuul.EnableZuulProxy;

@EnableZuulProxy
@SpringBootApplication
public class EdgeProxyApplication {
    public static void main(String[] args) {
        SpringApplication.run(EdgeProxyApplication.class, args);
    }
}
```

3. Create a file called `application.yml` in the `src/main/resources` directory of your application. This file will specify your route configurations. In this example, we'll imagine that our monolith application can be accessed on the `monolith.pichat-int.me` internal host and we want to expose the `/signup` and `/auth/login` paths to the public internet:

```
zuul:
 routes:
  signup:
   path: /signup
   url: http://monolith.pichat-int.me
  auth:
   path: /auth/login
   url: http://monolith.pichat-int.me
```

4. Start the project with `./gradlew bootRun` and you should be able to access the `/signup` and `/auth/login` URLs, which will be proxied to our monolith application.

5. We want to expose the `attachment-service` URLs to the internet. The attachment service exposes the following endpoints:

```
POST / # Creates an attachment
GET / # Fetch attachments, can filter by message_id
DELETE /:attachment_id # Deletes the specified attachment
GET /:id # Get the specific attachment
```

6. We'll need to decide which paths we want to use in our public API. Modify `application.properties` to add the following entries:

```
zuul:
 routes:
  signup:
   path: /signup
   url: http://monolith.pichat-int.me
  auth:
   path: /auth/login
   url: http://monolith.pichat-int.me
  attachments:
   path: /attachments/**
   url: http://attachment-service.pichat-int.me
```

7. Now all requests to `/attachments/*` will be forwarded to the attachment service and signup, and `auth/login` will continue to be served by our monolith application.

8. We can test this by running our service locally and sending requests to `localhost:8080/signup`, `localhost:8080/auth/login`, and `localhost:8080/attachments/foo`. You should be able to see that requests are routed to the respected services. Of course, the service will respond with an error because `attachment-service.pichat-int.me` cannot be resolved, but this shows that the routing is working as expected:

```
$ curl -D - http://localhost:8080/attachments/foo
HTTP/1.1 500
X-Application-Context: application
Content-Type: application/json;charset=UTF-8
Transfer-Encoding: chunked
Date: Tue, 27 Mar 2018 12:52:21 GMT
Connection: close

{"timestamp":1522155141889,"status":500,"error":"Internal Server
Error","exception":"com.netflix.zuul.exception.ZuulException","mess
age":"attachment-service.pichat-int.me"}%
```

Extending your services with sidecars

When you start developing microservices, it's common to embed a certain amount of boilerplate into each service. Logging, metrics, and configuration are all functionalities that are commonly copied from service to service, resulting in a large amount of boilerplate and copied and pasted code. As your architecture grows and you develop more services, this kind of setup becomes harder and harder to maintain. The usual result is that you end up with a bunch of different ways of doing logging, metrics, service discovery, and so on, which results in systems that are hard to debug and maintain. Changing something as simple as a metrics namespace or adding a feature to your service discovery clients can require the coordination of multiple teams and code bases. More realistically, your microservices architecture will continue to grow with inconsistent logging, metrics, and service discovery conventions, making it harder for developers to operate, contributing to overall operational pain.

The sidecar pattern describes a pattern whereby you extend the functionality of a service with a separate process or container running on the same machine. Common functionalities, such as metrics, logging, service discovery, configuration, or even network RPC, can be factored out of your application and handled by a sidecar service running alongside it. This pattern makes it easy to standardize shared concerns within your architecture by implementing them in a separate process that can be used by all of your services.

A common method for implementing a sidecar is to build a small, separate process that exposes some functionality over a commonly used protocol, such as HTTP. Imagine, for instance, that you want all of your services to use a centralized service-discovery service instead of relying on DNS hosts and ports to be set in each application's configuration. To accomplish this, you'd need to have up-to-date client libraries for your service-discovery service available in all of the languages that your services and monolith are written in. A better way would be to run a sidecar parallel to each service that runs a service-discovery client. Your services could then proxy requests to the sidecar and have it determine where to send them. As an added benefit, you could configure the sidecar to emit consistent metrics around network RPC requests made between services.

This is such a common pattern that there are multiple open source solutions available for it. In this recipe, we'll use `spring-cloud-netflix-sidecar`, a project that includes a simple HTTP API that allows non-JVM applications to use JVM client libraries. The Netflix sidecar assumes you are using Eureka, a service registry designed to support the service-discovery needs of clients. We'll discuss service discovery in more detail in later chapters. The sidecar also assumes your non-JVM application is serving a health-check endpoint and will use this to advertise its health to Eureka. Our Rails application exposes such an endpoint, /health, which, when running normally, will return a small JSON payload with a key status and the UP value.

How to do it...

1. Start by creating a basic Spring Boot service. Include the Spring Boot Gradle plugin and add dependencies for Spring Boot and the Spring Cloud Netflix sidecar project:

```
group 'com.packtpub.microservices'
version '1.0-SNAPSHOT'

buildscript {
    repositories {
        mavenCentral()
    }
    dependencies {
        classpath "org.springframework.boot:spring-boot-gradle-
plugin:1.4.4.RELEASE"
        classpath "io.spring.gradle:dependency-management-
plugin:0.5.6.RELEASE"
    }
}

apply plugin: 'java'
```

```
apply plugin: 'org.springframework.boot'
apply plugin: 'io.spring.dependency-management'

sourceCompatibility = 1.8

repositories {
    mavenCentral()
}

dependencyManagement {
    imports {
        mavenBom 'org.springframework.cloud:spring-cloud-
netflix:1.4.4.RELEASE'
    }
}

dependencies {
    compile group: 'org.springframework.boot', name: 'spring-boot-
starter-web', version: '1.4.4.RELEASE'
    compile group: 'org.springframework.cloud', name: 'spring-
cloud-netflix-sidecar', version: '1.4.4.RELEASE'
    testCompile group: 'junit', name: 'junit', version: '4.12'
}
```

2. We're ready to create a simple Spring Boot application. We'll use the `@EnableSidecar` annotation, which also includes the `@EnableZuulProxy`, `@EnableCircuitBreaker`, and `@EnableDiscoveryClient` annotations:

```
package com.packtpub.microservices;

import org.springframework.boot.SpringApplication;
import
org.springframework.boot.autoconfigure.EnableAutoConfiguration;
import org.springframework.cloud.netflix.sidecar.EnableSidecar;
import org.springframework.stereotype.Controller;

@EnableSidecar
@Controller
@EnableAutoConfiguration
public class SidecarController {
    public static void main(String[] args) {
        SpringApplication.run(SidecarController.class, args);
    }
}
```

3. The Netflix sidecar application requires a few configuration settings to be present. Create a new file called `application.yml` with the following content:

```
server:
 port: 5678

sidecar:
 port: 3000
 health-uri: http://localhost:3000/health
```

4. The sidecar will now expose an API that allows non-JVM applications to locate services registered with Eureka. If our `attachment-service` is registered with Eureka, the sidecar will proxy requests to
`http://localhost:5678/attachment/1234` to
`http://attachment-service.pichat-int.me/1234`.

Using API Gateways for routing requests to services

As we've seen in other recipes, microservices should provide a specific business capability and should be designed around one or more domain concepts, surrounded by a bounded context. This approach to designing service boundaries works well to guide you toward simple, independently-scalable services that can be managed and deployed by a single team dedicated to a certain area of your application or business.

When designing user interfaces, clients often aggregate related but distinct entities from various backend microservices. In our fictional messaging application, for instance, the screen that shows an actual message might have information from a message service, a media service, a likes service, a comments service, and so on. All of this information can be cumbersome to collect and can result in a large number of round-trip requests to the backend.

Porting a web application from a monolith with server-side-rendered HTML to a single-page JavaScript application, for example, can easily result in hundreds of `XMLHttpRequests` for a single page load:

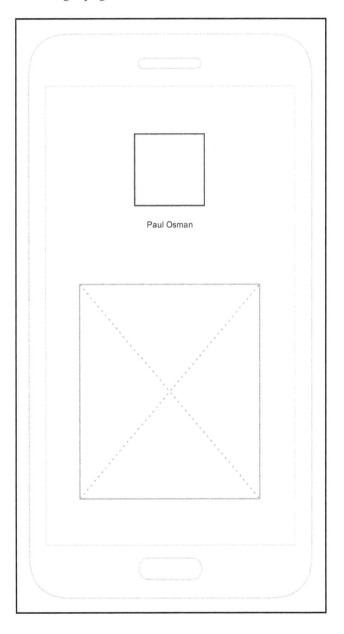

To reduce the amount of round-trip requests to the backend services, consider creating one or more API Gateways that provide an API that is catered to the client's needs. API Gateways can be used to present a single view of backend entities in a way that makes it easier for clients who use the API. In the preceding example, a request to a single message endpoint could return information about the message itself, media included in the message, likes and comments, and other information.

These entities can be concurrently collected from various backend services using a fan-out request pattern:

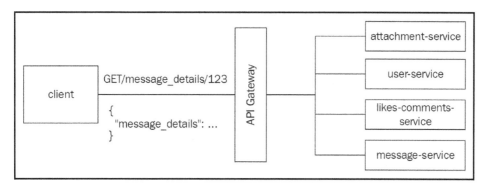

Design considerations

One of the benefits of using an API Gateway to provide access to microservices is that you can create a single, cohesive API for a specific client. In most cases, you'll want to create a specific API for mobile clients, perhaps even one API for iOS and one for Android. This implementation of API Gateways is commonly referred to as the **Backend for Frontend** (**BFF**) because it provides a single logical backend for each frontend application. A web application has very different needs than a mobile device.

In our situation, we'll focus on creating one endpoint that provides all the data needed by the message-view screen. This includes the message itself as well as the attachment(s), the user details of the sender, and any additional recipients of the message. If the message is public, it can also have likes and comments, which we'll imagine are served by a separate service. Our endpoint could look something like this:

```
GET /message_details/:message_id
```

The endpoint will return a response similar to the following:

```json
{
  "message_details": {
    "message": {
      "id": 1234,
      "body": "Hi There!",
      "from_user_id": "user:4321"
    },
    "attachments": [{
      "id": 4543,
      "media_type": 1,
      "url": "http://..."
    }],
    "from_user": {
      "username": "paulosman",
      "profile_pic": "http://...",
      "display_name": "Paul Osman"
    },
    "recipients": [
      ...
    ],
    "likes": 200,
    "comments": [{
      "id": 943,
      "body": "cool pic",
      "user": {
        "username": "somebody",
        "profile_pic": "http://..."
      }
    }]
  }
}
```

This response should have everything a client needs to show our message-view screen. The data itself comes from a variety of services, but, as we'll see, our API Gateway does the hard work of making those requests and aggregating the responses.

How to do it...

An API Gateway is responsible for exposing an API, making multiple service calls, aggregating the results, and returning them to the client. The **Finagle Scala** framework makes this natural by representing service calls as futures, which can be composed to represent dependencies. To stay consistent with other examples in this book, we'll build a small example gateway service in Java using the Spring Boot framework:

1. Create the project skeleton. Create a new Java project and add the following
   dependencies and plugins to the Gradle build file. We'll be using Spring Boot
   and Hystrix in this recipe:

```
plugins {
    id 'org.springframework.boot' version '1.5.9.RELEASE'
}

group 'com.packtpub.microservices'
version '1.0-SNAPSHOT'

apply plugin: 'java'

sourceCompatibility = 1.8

repositories {
    mavenCentral()
}

dependencies {
    compile group: 'org.springframework.boot', name: 'spring-boot-
starter-web', version: '1.5.9.RELEASE'
    compile group: 'com.netflix.hystrix', name: 'hystrix-core',
version: '1.0.2'
    testCompile group: 'junit', name: 'junit', version: '4.12'
}
```

Looking at the JSON example in the previous section, it's clear that we are
collecting and aggregating some distinct domain concepts. For the purposes of
this example, we'll imagine that we have a message service that retrieves
information about messages, including likes, comments, and attachments, and a
user service. Our gateway service will be making a call to the message service to
retrieve the message itself, then calls to the other services to get the associated
data, which we'll stitch together in a single response. For the purposes of this
recipe, imagine the message service is running on port 4567 and the user service
on port 4568. We'll create some stub services to mock out the data for these
hypothetical microservices.

2. Create a model to represent our Message data:

```
package com.packtpub.microservices.gateway.models;

import com.fasterxml.jackson.annotation.JsonIgnoreProperties;
import com.fasterxml.jackson.annotation.JsonProperty;

@JsonIgnoreProperties(ignoreUnknown = false)
```

```java
public class Message {

    private String id;
    private String body;

    @JsonProperty("from_user_id")
    private String fromUserId;

    public String getId() {
        return id;
    }

    public void setId(String id) {
        this.id = id;
    }

    public String getBody() {
        return body;
    }

    public void setBody(String body) {
        this.body = body;
    }

    public String getFromUserId() {
        return fromUserId;
    }

    public void setFromUserId(String fromUserId) {
        this.fromUserId = fromUserId;
    }
}
```

It's important that non-dependent service calls be done in a non-blocking, asynchronous manner. Luckily, Hystrix has an option to execute commands asynchronously, returning `Future<T>`.

3. Create a new package, say, `com.packtpub.microservices.gateway.commands` with the following classes:

   - Create the `AttachmentCommand` class with the following content:

   ```java
   package com.packtpub.microservices.gateway.commands;

   import com.netflix.hystrix.HystrixCommand;
   import com.netflix.hystrix.HystrixCommandGroupKey;
   ```

```
import org.springframework.http.ResponseEntity;
import org.springframework.web.client.RestTemplate;

public class AttachmentCommand extends HystrixCommand<String> {
    private String messageId;

    public AttachmentCommand(String messageId) {
super(HystrixCommandGroupKey.Factory.asKey("AttachmentCommand"));
        this.messageId = messageId;
    }

    @Override
    public String run() {
        RestTemplate template = new RestTemplate();
        String attachmentsUrl = "http://localhost:4567/message/" +
messageId + "/attachments";
        ResponseEntity<String> response =
template.getForEntity(attachmentsUrl, String.class);
        return response.getBody();
    }
}
```

- Create the `CommentCommand` class with the following content:

```
package com.packtpub.microservices.commands;

import com.netflix.hystrix.HystrixCommand;
import com.netflix.hystrix.HystrixCommandGroupKey;
import org.springframework.http.ResponseEntity;
import org.springframework.web.client.RestTemplate;

public class CommentCommand extends HystrixCommand<String> {

    private String messageId;

    public CommentCommand(String messageId) {
super(HystrixCommandGroupKey.Factory.asKey("CommentGroup"));
        this.messageId = messageId;
    }

    @Override
    public String run() {
        RestTemplate template = new RestTemplate();
        String commentsUrl = "http://localhost:4567/message/" +
messageId + "/comments";
        ResponseEntity<String> response =
template.getForEntity(commentsUrl, String.class);
        return response.getBody();
```

```
        }
    }
```

- Create the `LikeCommand` class with the following content:

```java
package com.packtpub.microservices.commands;

import com.netflix.hystrix.HystrixCommand;
import com.netflix.hystrix.HystrixCommandGroupKey;
import org.springframework.http.ResponseEntity;
import org.springframework.web.client.RestTemplate;

public class LikeCommand extends HystrixCommand<String> {

    private String messageId;

    public LikeCommand(String messageId) {
        super(HystrixCommandGroupKey.Factory.asKey("Likegroup"));
        this.messageId = messageId;
    }

    @Override
    public String run() {
        RestTemplate template = new RestTemplate();
        String likesUrl = "http://localhost:4567/message/" +
messageId + "/likes";
        ResponseEntity<String> response =
template.getForEntity(likesUrl, String.class);
        return response.getBody();
    }
}
```

- Our `MessageClient` class is a bit different than the previous examples—instead of returning the JSON string from the service response, it'll return an object representation, in this case, an instance of our `Message` class:

```java
package com.packtpub.microservices.commands;

import com.netflix.hystrix.HystrixCommand;
import com.netflix.hystrix.HystrixCommandGroupKey;
import com.packtpub.microservices.models.Message;
import org.springframework.web.client.RestTemplate;

public class MessageClient extends HystrixCommand<Message> {

    private final String id;
```

```
    public MessageClient(String id) {
super(HystrixCommandGroupKey.Factory.asKey("MessageGroup"));
        this.id = id;
    }

    @Override
    public Message run() {
        RestTemplate template = new RestTemplate();
        String messageServiceUrl = "http://localhost:4567/message/"
+ id;
        Message message = template.getForObject(messageServiceUrl,
Message.class);
        return message;
    }
}
```

- Create the UserCommand class with the following content:

```
package com.packtpub.microservices.commands;

import com.netflix.hystrix.HystrixCommand;
import com.netflix.hystrix.HystrixCommandGroupKey;
import org.springframework.http.ResponseEntity;
import org.springframework.web.client.RestTemplate;

public class UserCommand extends HystrixCommand<String> {

    private String id;

    public UserCommand(String id) {
        super(HystrixCommandGroupKey.Factory.asKey("UserGroup"));
        this.id = id;
    }

    @Override
    public String run() {
        RestTemplate template = new RestTemplate();
        String userServiceUrl = "http://localhost:4568/user/" + id;
        ResponseEntity<String> response =
template.getForEntity(userServiceUrl, String.class);
        return response.getBody();
    }
}
```

4. Stitch together the execution of these Hystrix commands in a single controller that exposes our API as the `/message_details/:message_id` endpoint:

```java
package com.packtpub.microservices;

import com.fasterxml.jackson.databind.ObjectMapper;
import com.packtpub.microservices.commands.*;
import com.packtpub.microservices.models.Message;
import org.springframework.boot.SpringApplication;
import org.springframework.http.MediaType;
import
org.springframework.boot.autoconfigure.SpringBootApplication;
import org.springframework.web.bind.annotation.PathVariable;
import org.springframework.web.bind.annotation.RequestMapping;
import org.springframework.web.bind.annotation.RestController;

import java.io.IOException;
import java.io.StringWriter;
import java.util.HashMap;
import java.util.Map;
import java.util.concurrent.ExecutionException;
import java.util.concurrent.Future;

@SpringBootApplication
@RestController
public class MainController {

    @RequestMapping(value = "/message_details/{id}", produces =
MediaType.APPLICATION_JSON_UTF8_VALUE)
    public Map<String, HashMap<String, String>>
messageDetails(@PathVariable String id)
            throws ExecutionException, InterruptedException,
IOException {

        Map<String, HashMap<String, String>> result = new
HashMap<>();
        HashMap<String, String> innerResult = new HashMap<>();

        Message message = new MessageClient(id).run();
        String messageId = message.getId();

        Future<String> user = new
UserClient(message.getFromUserId()).queue();
        Future<String> attachments = new
AttachmentClient(messageId).queue();
        Future<String> likes = new LikeClient(messageId).queue();
        Future<String> comments = new
CommentClient(messageId).queue();
```

```java
        ObjectMapper mapper = new ObjectMapper();
        StringWriter writer = new StringWriter();
        mapper.writeValue(writer, message);

        innerResult.put("message", writer.toString());
        innerResult.put("from_user", user.get());
        innerResult.put("attachments", attachments.get());
        innerResult.put("comments", comments.get());
        innerResult.put("likes", likes.get());

        result.put("message_details", innerResult);

        return result;
    }

    public static void main(String[] args) {
        SpringApplication.run(MainController.class, args);
    }
}
```

5. There you have it. Run the service with `./gradlew bootRun` and test it by making a request to:

```
$ curl -H "Content-Type: application/json"
http://localhost:8080/message_details/1234
```

Stopping cascading failures with Hystrix

Failures in a complex system can be hard to diagnose. Often, the symptom can appear far away from the cause. Users might start experiencing higher-than-normal error rates during login because of some downstream service that manages profile pictures or something else tangentially related to user profiles. An error in one service can often propagate needlessly to a user request and adversely impact user experience and therefore trust in your application. Additionally, a failing service can have cascading effects, turning a small system outage into a high-severity, customer-impacting incident. It's important when designing microservices to consider failure isolation and decide how you want to handle different failure scenarios.

A number of patterns can be used to improve the resiliency of distributed systems. Circuit breakers are a common pattern used to back off from making requests to a temporarily overwhelmed service. Circuit breakers were first described in Michael Nygard's book *Release It!*. A calling service defaults to a closed state, meaning requests are sent to the downstream service.

If the calling service receives too many failures too quickly, it can change the state of its circuit breaker to open, and start failing fast. Instead of waiting for the downstream service to fail again and adding to the load of the failing service, it just sends an error to upstream services, giving the overwhelmed service time to recover. After a certain amount of time has passed, the circuit is closed again and requests start flowing to the downstream service.

There are many available frameworks and libraries that implement circuit breakers. Some frameworks, such as Twitter's Finagle, automatically wrap every RPC call in a circuit breaker. In our example, we'll use the popular Netflix library, hystrix. Hystrix is a general-purpose, fault-tolerance library that structures isolated code as commands. When a command is executed, it checks the state of a circuit breaker to decide whether to issue or short circuit the request.

How to do it...

Hystrix is made available as a Java library, so we'll demonstrate its use by building a small Java Spring Boot application:

1. Create a new Java application and add the dependencies to your build.gradle file:

```
plugins {
    id 'org.springframework.boot' version '1.5.9.RELEASE'
}

group 'com.packetpub.microservices'
version '1.0-SNAPSHOT'

apply plugin: 'java'

sourceCompatibility = 1.8

repositories {
    mavenCentral()
}

dependencies {
    compile group: 'org.springframework.boot', name: 'spring-boot-
starter-web', version: '1.5.9.RELEASE'
    compile group: 'com.netflix.hystrix', name: 'hystrix-core',
version: '1.0.2'
    testCompile group: 'junit', name: 'junit', version: '4.12'
}
```

2. We'll create a simple `MainController` that returns a simple message. This is a contrived example, but it demonstrates an upstream service making downstream calls. At first, our application will just return a hardcoded `Hello, World!` message. Next, we'll move the string out to a Hystrix command. Finally, we'll move the message to a service call wrapped in a Hystrix command:

```
package com.packtpub.microservices;

import org.springframework.boot.SpringApplication;
import
org.springframework.boot.autoconfigure.EnableAutoConfiguration;
import
org.springframework.boot.autoconfigure.SpringBootApplication;
import org.springframework.web.bind.annotation.RequestMapping;
import org.springframework.web.bind.annotation.RestController;

@SpringBootApplication
@EnableAutoConfiguration
@RestController
public class MainController {
    @RequestMapping("/message")
    public String message() {
        return "Hello, World!";
    }

    public static void main(String[] args) {
        SpringApplication.run(MainController.class, args);
    }
}
```

3. Move the message out to `HystrixCommand`:

```
package com.packtpub.microservices;

import com.netflix.hystrix.HystrixCommand;
import com.netflix.hystrix.HystrixCommandGroupKey;

public class CommandHelloWorld extends HystrixCommand<String> {

    private String name;

    CommandHelloWorld(String name) {
super(HystrixCommandGroupKey.Factory.asKey("ExampleGroup"));
        this.name = name;
    }

    @Override
```

```
        public String run() {
            return "Hello, " + name + "!";
        }
    }
```

4. Replace the method in `MainController` to use `HystrixCommand`:

```
@RequestMapping("/message")
public String message() {
    return new CommandHelloWorld("Paul").execute();
}
```

5. Move the message generation to another service. We're hardcoding the hypothetical message service URL here, which is not a good practice but will do for demonstration purposes:

```
package com.packtpub.microservices;

import com.netflix.hystrix.HystrixCommand;
import com.netflix.hystrix.HystrixCommandGroupKey;
import org.springframework.http.ResponseEntity;
import org.springframework.web.client.RestTemplate;

public class CommandHelloWorld extends HystrixCommand<String> {

    CommandHelloWorld() {
    super(HystrixCommandGroupKey.Factory.asKey("ExampleGroup"));
    }

    @Override
    public String run() {
        RestTemplate restTemplate = new RestTemplate();
        String messageResourceUrl = "http://localhost:4567/";
        ResponseEntity<String> response =
restTemplate.getForEntity(messageResourceUrl, String.class);
        return response.getBody();
    }

    @Override
    public String getFallback() {
        return "Hello, Fallback Message";
    }
}
```

6. Update the `MainController` class to contain the following:

```
package com.packetpub.microservices;

import org.springframework.boot.SpringApplication;
import
org.springframework.boot.autoconfigure.EnableAutoConfiguration;
import
org.springframework.boot.autoconfigure.SpringBootApplication;
import org.springframework.web.bind.annotation.RequestMapping;
import org.springframework.web.bind.annotation.RestController;

@SpringBootApplication
@EnableAutoConfiguration
@RestController
public class MainController {

    @RequestMapping("/message")
    public String message() {
        return new CommandHelloWorld().execute();
    }

    public static void main(String[] args) {
        SpringApplication.run(MainController.class, args);
    }

}
```

7. Our `MainController` class now makes a service call, wrapped in a Hystrix command, to generate a message to send back to the client. You can test this by creating a very simple service that generates a message string. `sinatra` is a simple-to-use Ruby library ideal for creating test services. Create a new file called `message-service.rb`:

```
require 'sinatra'

get '/' do
  "Hello from Sinatra"
end
```

8. Run the service by running `ruby message-service.rb` and then make a few sample requests to your Hystrix-enabled service. You can simulate a failure by modifying the service to return a `503`, indicating that it is temporarily overwhelmed:

```
require 'sinatra'

get '/' do
  halt 503, 'Busy'
end
```

Your Spring service should now attempt to reach the service but use the value in the fallback when it encounters a `503`. Furthermore, after a number of attempts, the command's circuit breaker will be tripped and the service will start defaulting to the fallback for a period of time.

Rate limiting

In addition to techniques such as circuit breaking, rate limiting can be an effective way to prevent cascading failures in a distributed system. Rate limiting can be effective at preventing spam, protecting against **Denial of Service (DoS)** attacks, and protecting parts of a system from becoming overloaded by too many simultaneous requests. Typically implemented as either a global or per-client limit, rate limiting is usually part of a proxy or load balancer. In this recipe, we'll use NGINX, a popular open source load balancer, web server, and reverse proxy.

Most rate-limiting implementations use the *leaky-bucket algorithm*—an algorithm that originated in computer network switches and telecommunications networks. As the name suggests, the leaky-bucket algorithm is based on the metaphor of a bucket with a small leak in it that controls a constant rate. Water is poured into the bucket in bursts, but the leak guarantees that water exists in the bucket at a steady, fixed rate. If the water is poured in faster than the water exits the bucket, eventually the bucket will overflow. In this case, the overflow represents requests that are dropped.

It's certainly possible to implement your own rate-limiting solution; there are even implementations of the algorithms out there that are open source and available to use. It's a lot easier, however, to use a product such as NGINX to do rate limiting for you. In this recipe, we'll configure NGINX to proxy requests to our microservice.

How to do it...

1. Install NGINX by running the following command:

```
apt-get install nginx
```

2. nginx has a config file, nginx.conf. On an Ubuntu-based Linux system, this will probably be in the /etc/nginx/nginx.conf directory. Open the file and look for the http block and add the following content:

```
limit_req_zone $binary_remote_addr zone=mylimit:10m rate=10r/s;
server {
    location /auth/signin {
        limit_req zone=mylimit;
        proxy_pass http://my_upstream;
    }
}
```

As you can see from the preceding code, rate limiting is implemented with two configuration directives. The limit_req_zone directive defines the parameters for rate limiting. In this example, we're implementing a rate limit, based on the client's IP address, of 10 requests per second. The limit_req directive applies our rate limiting to a specific path or location. In this case, we're applying it to all requests to /auth/signin, presumably because we don't want bots scripting the creation of accounts!

Using service mesh for shared concerns

As web services' frameworks and standards evolve, the amount of boilerplate or shared application concerns is reduced. This is because, collectively, we figure out what parts of our applications are universal and therefore shouldn't need to be re-implemented by every programmer or team. When people first started networking computers, programmers writing network-aware applications had to worry about a lot of low-level details that are now abstracted out by the operating system's networking stack. Similarly, there are certain universal concerns that all microservices share. Frameworks such as Twitter's Finagle wrap all network calls in a circuit breaker, increasing fault tolerance and isolating failures in systems. Finagle and Spring Boot, the Java framework we've been using for most of these recipes, both support exposing a standard metrics endpoint that standardizes basic network, JVM, and application metrics collected for microservices.

Every microservice should consider a number of shared application concerns. From an observability perspective, services should strive to emit consistent metrics and structured logs. To improve the reliability of our systems, services should wrap network calls in circuit breakers and implement consistent retry and back-off logic. To support changes in network and service topology, services should consider implementing client-side load balancing and use centralized service discovery.

Instead of implementing all of these features in each of our services, it would be ideal to abstract them out to something outside our application code that could be maintained and operated separately. Like the features of our operating systems network stack, if each of these features is implemented by something our application could rely on being present, we would not have to worry about them being available. This is the idea behind a service mesh.

Running a service mesh configuration involves running each microservice in your system behind a network proxy. Instead of services speaking directly to one another, they communicate via their respective proxies, which are installed as sidecars. Practically speaking, your service would communicate with its own proxy running on localhost. As network requests are sent through a services proxy, the proxy can control what metrics are emitted and what log messages are output. The proxy can also integrate directly with your service registry and distribute requests evenly among active nodes, keeping track of failures and opting to fail fast when a certain threshold has been reached. Running your system in this kind of configuration can ease the operational complexity of your system while improving the reliability and observability of your architecture.

Like most of the recipes discussed in this chapter, there are numerous open source solutions for running a service mesh. We'll focus on **Linkerd**, an open source proxy server built and maintained by buoyant. The original authors of Linkerd worked at Twitter before forming buoyant and as such, Linkerd incorporates many of the lessons learned by teams at Twitter. It shares many features with the Finagle Scala framework, but can be used with services written in any language. In this recipe, we'll walk through installing and configuring Linkerd and discuss how we can use it to control communication between our Ruby on Rails monolith API and our newly developed media service.

How to do it...

To demonstrate running a service behind a proxy, we'll install and run an instance of Linkerd and configure it to handle requests to and from your service. There are instructions on the Linkerd website for running it in Docker, Kubernetes, and other options. To keep things simple, we'll focus on running Linkerd and our service locally:

1. Download the latest Linkerd release at `https://github.com/linkerd/linkerd/releases`.

2. Extract the tarball by executing the following command:

   ```
   $ tar xvfz linkerd-1.3.4.tgz
   $ cd linkerd-1.3.4
   ```

3. By default, `linkerd` ships with a configuration that uses file-based service discovery. We'll discuss alternatives to this approach next, but, for now, create a new file called `disco/media-service` with the following contents:

   ```
   localhost 8080
   ```

4. This maps the hostname and port to a service called `media-service`. Linkerd uses this file to look up services by name and determines the hostname and port mappings.

5. Run Linkerd as follows:

   ```
   $ ./linkerd-1.3.4-exec config/linkerd.yaml
   ```

6. Start the service on port `8080`. Change into the `media-service` directory and run the service:

   ```
   $ ./gradlew bootRun
   ```

7. Linkerd is running on port `4140`. Test that proxying is working with the following request:

   ```
   $ curl -H "Host: attachment-service" http://localhost:4140/
   ```

Inter-service Communication 3

In this chapter, we will cover the following recipes:

- Service-to-service communication
- Making concurrent asynchronous requests
- Finding services using service discovery
- Server-side load balancing
- Client-side load balancing
- Building event-driven microservices
- Evolving APIs

Introduction

In the previous chapters, we've covered how to begin breaking a monolithic codebase into microservices, as well as best practices for exposing your microservices to the public internet. So far, we've assumed that all of our microservices are standalone applications that have no dependencies. These simple microservices receive requests, retrieve data or write to a database, and return a response to clients. This kind of linear workflow is rare in real-world systems. In a real-world microservice architecture, services will frequently need to invoke other services in order to fulfill a user's request. A typical user request will commonly create dozens of requests to services in your system.

Managing the communication between services presents a number of challenges. Before a service can speak to another service, it will need to locate it through some kind of service-discovery mechanism. When generating requests to a downstream service, we also need a way to distribute traffic across the various instances of the service that minimizes latency and distributes the load evenly without compromising data integrity. We'll need to consider how to handle service failures and prevent them from cascading throughout our system.

Sometimes a service will need to communicate with other services asynchronously, in these cases, we can use event-driven architectural patterns to create reactive workflows. Breaking our system up into multiple services also means that different services will evolve their APIs independently, so we'll need ways to handle changes that won't break upstream services.

In this chapter, we'll discuss recipes designed to address each of these challenges. By the end of this chapter, you'll be able to confidently handle the various kinds of interactions we're bound to require in a microservice architecture.

Service-to-service communication

In large-scale systems, problems arise less often in services themselves and more often in the communication between services. For this reason, we need to carefully consider all of the various challenges in service-to-service communication. When discussing service-to-service communication, it's useful to visualize the flow of information in our system. Data flows in both directions–from the client (upstream) to the database, or event bus (downstream) in the form of requests, and back again in the form of responses. When we refer to upstream services, we are describing components of the system that are closer to the user in the flow of information. When we refer to downstream services, we are describing components of the system that are further away from the user–in other words, the user makes a request that is routed to a service that then makes requests to other, downstream services, as shown in the following diagram:

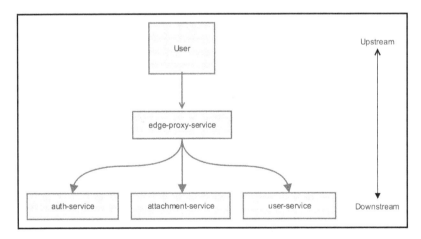

In the preceding diagram, the originating **User** is upstream from the **edge-proxy-service**, which is upstream from the **auth-service**, **attachment-service**, and **user-service**.

In order to demonstrate the service-to-service communication, we'll create a simple service that calls another service synchronously using the Spring Boot Java framework. Keeping with the example of our fictional messaging application, we'll create a message service that is responsible for sending messages. The message service has to invoke the social graph service in order to determine whether the sender and recipient of a message are friends before allowing a message to be sent. The following simplified diagram illustrates the relationship between services:

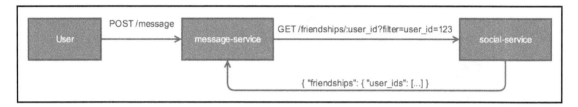

As you can see, a **POST** request comes in from the user to the **/message** endpoint, which is routed to **message-service**. The **message-service** service then makes an HTTP **GET** request to the **social-service** service using the **/friendships/:id** endpoint. The **social-service** service returns a JSON representation of friendships for a user.

How to do it...

1. Create a new Java/Gradle project called `message-service` and add the following content to the `build.gradle` file:

```
group 'com.packtpub.microservices'
version '1.0-SNAPSHOT'

buildscript {
    repositories {
        mavenCentral()
    }
    dependencies {
        classpath group: 'org.springframework.boot', name: 'spring-boot-gradle-plugin', version: '1.5.9.RELEASE'
    }
}

apply plugin: 'java'
apply plugin: 'org.springframework.boot'

sourceCompatibility = 1.8
```

```
repositories {
    mavenCentral()
}

dependencies {
    compile group: 'org.springframework.boot', name: 'spring-boot-
    starter-web'
    testCompile group: 'junit', name: 'junit', version: '4.12'
}
```

2. Create a new package called com.packtpub.microservices.ch03.message and a new class called Application. This will be our service's entry point:

```
package com.packtpub.microservices.ch03.message;

import org.springframework.boot.SpringApplication;
import
org.springframework.boot.autoconfigure.SpringBootApplication;

@SpringBootApplication
public class Application {
    public static void main(String[] args) {
        SpringApplication.run(Application.class, args);
    }
}
```

3. Create the model. Create a package called
   com.packtpub.microservices.ch03.message.models and a class called
   Message. This is the internal representation of the message. There's a lot missing
   here. We're not actually persisting the message in this code, as it's best to keep
   this example simple:

```
package com.packtpub.microservices.ch03.message.models;

public class Message {

    private String toUser;
    private String fromUser;
    private String body;

    public Message() {}

    public Message(String toUser, String fromUser, String body) {
        this.toUser = toUser;
        this.fromUser = fromUser;
        this.body = body;
    }
```

```
    public String getToUser() {
        return toUser;
    }

    public String getFromUser() {
        return fromUser;
    }

    public String getBody() {
        return body;
    }
}
```

4. Create a new package called
   `com.packtpub.microservices.ch03.message.controllers` and a new
   class called `MessageController`. At the moment, our controller doesn't do
   much except accept the request, parse the JSON, and return the message instance,
   as you can see from this code:

```
package com.packtpub.microservices.ch03.message.controllers;

import com.packtpub.microservices.models.Message;
import org.springframework.web.bind.annotation.*;

@RestController
public class MessageController {

    @RequestMapping(
            path="/messages",
            method=RequestMethod.POST,
            produces="application/json")
    public Message create(@RequestBody Message message) {
        return message;
    }
}
```

5. Test this basic service by running it and trying to send a simple request:

```
$ ./gradlew bootRun
Starting a Gradle Daemon, 1 busy Daemon could not be reused, use --
status for details

> Task :bootRun

  .   ____          _            __ _ _
 /\\ / ___'_ __ _ _(_)_ __  __ _ \ \ \ \
( ( )\___ | '_ | '_| | '_ \/ _` | \ \ \ \
 \\/  ___)| |_)| | | | | || (_| |  ) ) ) )
  '  |____| .__|_| |_|_| |_\__, | / / / /
 =========|_|==============|___/=/_/_/_/
 :: Spring Boot ::        (v1.5.9.RELEASE)

...
```

Take a look at the following command line:

```
$ curl -H "Content-Type: application/json" -X POST
http://localhost:8080/messages -d'{"toUser": "reader", "fromUser":
"paulosman", "body": "Hello, World"}'

{"toUser":"reader","fromUser":"paulosman","body":"Hello, World"}
```

Now we have a basic service working, but it's pretty dumb and not doing much. We won't go into persistence in this chapter, but let's add some intelligence by checking with the social service to verify that our two users have a friendship before allowing the message to be sent. For the purposes of our example, imagine we have a working social service that allows us to check for relationships between users with requests, like so:

```
GET /friendships?username=paulosman&filter=reader

{
  "username": "paulosman",
  "friendships": [
    "reader"
  ]
}
```

6. Before we can consume this service, let's create a model to store its response. In the `com.packtpub.microservices.ch03.message.models` package, create a class called `UserFriendships`:

```
package com.packtpub.microservices.ch03.message.models;

import com.fasterxml.jackson.annotation.JsonIgnoreProperties;

import java.util.List;

@JsonIgnoreProperties(ignoreUnknown = true)
public class UserFriendships {
    private String username;
    private List<String> friendships;

    public UserFriendships() {}

    public String getUsername() {
        return username;
    }

    public void setUsername(String username) {
        this.username = username;
    }

    public List<String> getFriendships() {
        return friendships;
    }

    public void setFriendships(List<String> friendships) {
        this.friendships = friendships;
    }
}
```

7. Modify `MessageController`, adding a method to get a list of friendships for a user, optionally filtering by a username. Note that we're hardcoding the URL in this example, which is a bad practice. We'll discuss alternatives to this in the next recipe. Take a look at the following code:

```
private List<String> getFriendsForUser(String username, String
filter) {
    String url = "http://localhost:4567/friendships?username=" +
username + "&filter=" + filter;
    RestTemplate template = new RestTemplate();
```

```
        UserFriendships friendships = template.getForObject(url,
UserFriendships.class);
        return friendships.getFriendships();
    }
```

8. Modify the `create` method we wrote earlier. If the users are friends, we'll continue and return the message as before; if the users are not friends, the service will respond with a `403` indicating that the request is forbidden:

```
@RequestMapping(
            path="/messages",
            method=RequestMethod.POST,
            produces="application/json")
    public ResponseEntity<Message> create(@RequestBody Message
message) {
        List<String> friendships =
getFriendsForUser(message.getFromUser(), message.getToUser());

        if (friendships.isEmpty())
            return
ResponseEntity.status(HttpStatus.FORBIDDEN).build();

        URI location = ServletUriComponentsBuilder
                .fromCurrentRequest().path("/{id}")
                .buildAndExpand(message.getFromUser()).toUri();
        return ResponseEntity.created(location).build();
    }
```

Asynchronous requests

In the previous recipe, we were making a single service invocation per request, from the message service to the social service. This has the benefit of being incredibly simple to implement and, when using single-threaded languages, such as Python, Ruby, or JavaScript, is often the only choice. Performing a network call synchronously in this manner is acceptable when you're only doing it once per request–it doesn't matter that the call blocks the thread since you can't respond to the user until the invocation is complete anyway. When you're making multiple requests, however, blocking network calls will severely impact the performance and scalability of your application. What we need is an easy way to make use of Java's concurrency features.

If you're writing your microservices in Scala, you can take advantage of the `Future` type, which is used to represent an asynchronous computation. The **Finagle** RPC framework even uses futures as one of its base abstractions for modeling dependent RPCs. Java also has futures and the Spring Boot framework has some useful utilities that make it easy to wrap network calls, making them asynchronous and therefore non-blocking.

In this recipe, we'll retool the message service we introduced in the previous recipe. Instead of checking to see whether the sender and recipient of a message are friends, we'll now imagine that our app uses an asymmetric following model. For a user to message another user, the two users will have to follow each other. This requires the message service to make two network calls to the social service, checking that the sender follows the recipient and simultaneously checking that the recipient follows the sender. The following simplified diagram represents the relationship between services:

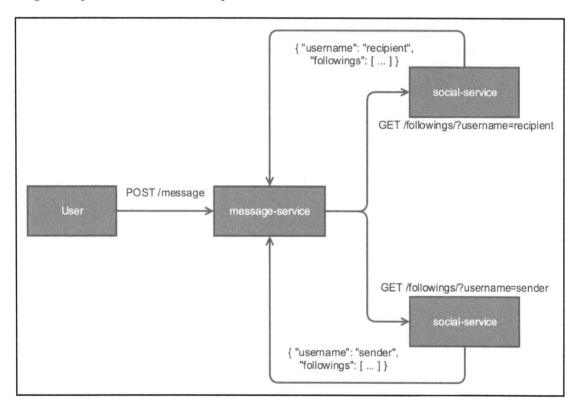

Spring Boot has useful tools that we can use to make methods asynchronous using Java's `CompletableFuture` type. We'll modify our previous message service to make two concurrent calls to the search service.

How to do it...

1. Open the `MessageController` file and insert the following content:

```
package com.packtpub.microservices.ch03.message.controllers;

import com.packtpub.microservices.models.Message;
import com.packtpub.microservices.models.UserFriendships;
import org.springframework.http.HttpStatus;
import org.springframework.http.ResponseEntity;
import org.springframework.web.bind.annotation.*;
import org.springframework.web.client.RestTemplate;
import
org.springframework.web.servlet.support.ServletUriComponentsBuilder
;

import java.net.URI;
import java.util.List;

@RestController
public class MessageController {

    @RequestMapping(
            path="/messages",
            method=RequestMethod.POST,
            produces="application/json")
    public ResponseEntity<Message> create(@RequestBody Message
message) {
        List<String> friendships =
getFriendsForUser(message.getFromUser(), message.getToUser());

        if (friendships.isEmpty())
            return
ResponseEntity.status(HttpStatus.FORBIDDEN).build();

        URI location = ServletUriComponentsBuilder
                .fromCurrentRequest().path("/{id}")
                .buildAndExpand(message.getFromUser()).toUri();

        return ResponseEntity.created(location).build();
    }

    private List<String> getFriendsForUser(String username, String
filter) {
        String url = "http://localhost:4567/friendships?username="
+ username + "&filter=" + filter;
        RestTemplate template = new RestTemplate();
```

```
        UserFriendships friendships = template.getForObject(url,
    UserFriendships.class);
        return friendships.getFriendships();
    }
}
```

2. Replace the `getFriendsForUser` method with a new method, called `isFollowing`. We give the new method an `@Async` annotation, which tells Spring Boot that this method will be run in a different thread:

   ```
   import org.springframework.scheduling.annotation.Async;
   import java.util.concurrent.CompletableFuture;


   ...


   @Async
   public CompletableFuture<Boolean> isFollowing(String fromUser,
   String toUser) {

       String url = String.format(
         "http://localhost:4567/followings?user=%s&filter=%s",
         fromUser, toUser);

       RestTemplate template = new RestTemplate();
       UserFollowings followings = template.forObject(url,
   UserFollowings.class);

       return CompletableFuture.completedFuture(
           followings.getFollowings().isEmpty()
       );
   }
   ```

3. Modify the `create` method to make the two service invocations. We'll need to wait until they are both done before deciding how to proceed, but the two service calls will be made concurrently:

   ```
   @RequestMapping(
               path="/messages",
               method=RequestMethod.POST,
               produces="application/json")
       public ResponseEntity<Message> create(@RequestBody Message
   message) {

       CompletableFuture<Boolean> result1 =
   isFollowing(message.getFromUser(), message.getToUser());
       CompletableFuture<Boolean> result2 =
   isFollowing(message.getToUser(), message.getFromUser());
   ```

```
CompletableFuture.allOf(result1, result2).join();

// if both are not true, respond with a 403
if (!(result1.get() && result2.get()))
    ResponseEntity.status(HttpStatus.FORBIDDEN).build();

... // proceed

}
```

4. For the @Async annotation to schedule methods on separate threads, we need to configure an Executor. This is done in our Application class, as follows:

```
package com.packtpub.microservices;

import org.springframework.boot.SpringApplication;
import
org.springframework.boot.autoconfigure.SpringBootApplication;
import org.springframework.context.annotation.Bean;
import org.springframework.scheduling.annotation.EnableAsync;
import
org.springframework.scheduling.concurrent.ThreadPoolTaskExecutor;

import java.util.concurrent.Executor;

@SpringBootApplication
@EnableAsync
public class Application {

    public static void main(String[] args) {
        SpringApplication.run(Application.class, args).close();
    }

    @Bean
    public Executor asyncExecutor() {
        ThreadPoolTaskExecutor executor = new
ThreadPoolTaskExecutor();
        executor.setCorePoolSize(2);
        executor.setMaxPoolSize(2);
        executor.setQueueCapacity(500);
        executor.setThreadNamePrefix("SocialServiceCall-");
        executor.initialize();
        return executor;
    }


}
```

Our service now makes concurrent asynchronous calls to the social service in order to ensure that the sender and recipient of a message follow each other. We customize our `Async` scheduler with `Executor` defined as part of our application's configuration. We've configured our `ThreadPoolTaskExecutor` class to limit the number of threads to 2 and the queue size to 500. There are many factors to consider when configuring `Executor`, such as the amount of traffic you expect your service to receive and the average amount of time it takes for your service to serve a request. In this example, we'll leave it with these values.

Service discovery

Before services can invoke each other, they need to be able to find each other using some kind of service discovery mechanism. This means being able to translate a service name into a network location (IP address and port). Traditional applications maintained the network locations of services to send requests to, probably in a configuration file (or worse, hardcoded in the application code). This approach assumes that network locations are relatively static, which isn't going to be the case in modern, cloud-native applications. The topologies of microservice architectures are constantly changing. Nodes are being added and removed through auto-scaling, and we have to assume that some nodes will fail either completely or by serving requests with unacceptably high latency. As a microservice architecture grows, you'll need to consider a more feature-rich service-discovery mechanism.

When choosing a service-discovery mechanism, the datastore used to back your service registry is extremely important. You want a well-tested, battle-worn system. Apache **ZooKeeper** is an open source hierarchical key-value store commonly used for distributed locking, service discovery, maintaining configuration information, and other distributed coordination tasks. The development of ZooKeeper was in part motivated by a paper published by Google in 2006 that described **Chubby**, an internally-developed system for distributed lock storage. In this recipe, we'll use ZooKeeper to build a service-discovery mechanism.

Spring Cloud ZooKeeper is a project that provides easy ZooKeeper integration in Spring Boot applications.

How to do it...

For this recipe, there are two sets of steps, as shown in the next sections.

Registering with the service registry

This recipe requires a running ZooKeeper cluster. At a minimum, you will need a single ZooKeeper node running locally on your development machine. For instructions on installing and running ZooKeeper, please visit the excellent ZooKeeper documentation. Take a look at the following steps:

1. For this example, we'll create a service to handle the creation and retrieval of user accounts. Create a new Gradle Java application called `users-service` with the following `build.gradle` file:

```
group 'com.packtpub.microservices'
version '1.0-SNAPSHOT'

buildscript {
    repositories {
        mavenCentral()
    }
    dependencies {
        classpath group: 'io.spring.gradle', name: 'dependency-
management-plugin', version: '0.5.6.RELEASE'
        classpath group: 'org.springframework.boot', name: 'spring-
boot-gradle-plugin', version: '1.5.9.RELEASE'
    }
}

apply plugin: 'java'
apply plugin: 'org.springframework.boot'
apply plugin: "io.spring.dependency-management"

sourceCompatibility = 1.8

dependencyManagement {
    imports {
        mavenBom 'org.springframework.cloud:spring-cloud-zookeeper-
dependencies:1.1.1.RELEASE'
    }
}

repositories {
    mavenCentral()
}

dependencies {
    compile group: 'io.reactivex', name: 'rxjava', version: '1.1.5'
    compile group: 'org.springframework.boot', name: 'spring-boot-
starter-web'
```

```
    compile group: 'org.springframework.cloud', name: 'spring-
cloud-starter-zookeeper-discovery', version: '1.1.1.RELEASE'
    testCompile group: 'junit', name: 'junit', version: '4.12'
}
```

2. Because we've declared `spring-boot-starter-zookeeper-discovery` as a dependency, we have access to the necessary annotations to tell our application to register itself with a ZooKeeper service registry on startup. Create a new class called `Application`, which will serve as our service's entry point:

```
package com.packtpub.microservices.ch03.servicediscovery;

import org.springframework.boot.SpringApplication;
import
org.springframework.boot.autoconfigure.SpringBootApplication;
import
org.springframework.cloud.client.discovery.EnableDiscoveryClient;

@EnableDiscoveryClient
@SpringBootApplication
public class Application {
    public static void main(String[] args) {
        SpringApplication.run(Application.class, args);
    }
}
```

3. The application now attempts to connect to a ZooKeeper node, by default running on port 2181 on localhost. This default will work for local development, but will need to be changed in a production environment anyway. Add a file `src/resources/application.yml` with the following contents:

```
spring:
  cloud:
    zookeeper:
      connect-string: localhost:2181
```

4. To give your service a meaningful name in the service registry, modify the `application.yml` file and add the following content:

```
spring:
  cloud:
    zookeeper:
      connect-string: localhost:2181
    application:
      name: users-service
```

Finding services

Now that we have a service being registered with the service registry, we'll create another service to demonstrate using the Spring ZooKeeper `DiscoveryClient` to find a running instance of that service:

1. Open our previously created message-service client. Add the following lines to `build.gradle`:

```
group 'com.packtpub.microservices'
version '1.0-SNAPSHOT'

buildscript {
    repositories {
        mavenCentral()
    }
    dependencies {
        classpath group: 'io.spring.gradle', name: 'dependency-management-plugin', version: '0.5.6.RELEASE'
        classpath group: 'org.springframework.boot', name: 'spring-boot-gradle-plugin', version: '1.5.9.RELEASE'
    }
}

apply plugin: 'java'
apply plugin: 'org.springframework.boot'
apply plugin: 'io.spring.dependency-management'

sourceCompatibility = 1.8

dependencyManagement {
    imports {
        mavenBom 'org.springframework.cloud:spring-cloud-zookeeper-dependencies:1.1.1.RELEASE'
    }
}
```

```
repositories {
    mavenCentral()
}

dependencies {
    compile 'io.reactivex:rxjava:1.3.4'
    compile group: 'org.springframework.cloud', name: 'spring-
cloud-starter-zookeeper-discovery', version: '1.1.1.RELEASE'
    compile group: 'org.springframework.cloud', name: 'spring-
cloud-starter-feign', version: '1.2.5.RELEASE'
    compile group: 'org.springframework.kafka', name: 'spring-
kafka', version: '2.1.1.RELEASE'
    compile group: 'org.springframework.boot', name: 'spring-boot-
starter-web'
    testCompile group: 'junit', name: 'junit', version: '4.12'
}
```

2. We're using an HTTP client developed by Netflix, called **Feign**. Feign allows you to declaratively build HTTP clients and supports service discovery by default. Create a new file called `UsersClient.java` with the following content:

```java
package com.packtpub.microservices.ch03.servicediscovery.clients;

import org.springframework.beans.factory.annotation.Autowired;
import
org.springframework.cloud.client.discovery.EnableDiscoveryClient;
import org.springframework.cloud.netflix.feign.EnableFeignClients;
import org.springframework.cloud.netflix.feign.FeignClient;
import org.springframework.context.annotation.Configuration;
import org.springframework.web.bind.annotation.PathVariable;
import org.springframework.web.bind.annotation.RequestMapping;
import org.springframework.web.bind.annotation.RequestMethod;
import org.springframework.web.bind.annotation.ResponseBody;

import java.util.List;

@Configuration
@EnableFeignClients
@EnableDiscoveryClient
public class UsersClient {

    @Autowired
    private Client client;

    @FeignClient("users-service")
    interface Client {
        @RequestMapping(path = "/followings/{userId}", method =
RequestMethod.GET)
```

```
            @ResponseBody
            List<String> getFollowings(@PathVariable("userId") String
        userId);
            }

        public List<String> getFollowings(String userId) {
            return client.getFollowings(userId);
        }
    }
```

3. Open the `MessageController.java` file, and add an instance of `UsersClient` as a field:

```
package com.packtpub.microservices;
...
@RestController
public class MessagesController {
    ...
    @Autowired
    private UsersClient usersClient;
    ...
}
```

4. Instead of manually building the URL in the `isFollowing` method, we can use the Feign client to automatically get a list of friendships for a user, as follows:

```
@Async
public CompletableFuture<Boolean> isFollowing(String fromUser,
String toUser) {
    List<String> friends = usersClient.getFollowings(fromUser)
            .stream()
            .filter(toUser::equals)
            .collect(Collectors.toList());

    return CompletableFuture.completedFuture(friends.isEmpty());
}
```

Because we're using a service registry, we no longer have to worry about clunky configs holding onto hostname values that can change. Furthermore, we're in a position to start deciding how we want to distribute the load among available instances of a service.

Server-side load balancing

When thinking about distributing load across a cluster of servers running instances of an application, it's interesting to consider a brief (and incomplete) history of web application architectures. Some of the earliest web applications were static HTML pages hosted by a web server, such as Apache or similar web server daemon software. Gradually, applications became more dynamic, using technologies such as server-side scripts executed through CGI. Even dynamic applications were still files hosted and served directly by a web server daemon. This simple architecture worked for a long time. Eventually, however, as the amount of traffic an application received grew, a way to distribute load among identical stateless instances of an application was needed.

There are a number of techniques for load balancing, including round-robin DNS or DNS geolocation. The simplest and most common form of load balancing for microservices is to use a software program that forwards requests to one of a cluster of backend servers. There are a number of different ways load can be distributed, based on the specific load-balancing algorithm used by the load balancer we choose. Simple load-balancing algorithms include round-robin and random choice. More often, in real-world production applications, we'll opt for a load-balancing algorithm that takes reported metrics, such as load or the number of active connections, into account when choosing a node in a cluster to forward a request to.

There are a number of popular open source applications that can perform effective load balancing for microservices. **HAProxy** is a popular open source load balancer that can do TCP and HTTP load balancing. NGINX is a popular open source web server that can be effectively used as a reverse proxy, application server, load balancer, or even HTTP cache. Nowadays, more organizations are in positions to develop microservices that are deployed on cloud platforms, such as Amazon Web Services or Google Cloud Platform, which each have solutions for server-side load balancing.

AWS provides a load-balancing solution called **Elastic Load Balancing** (**ELB**). ELB can be configured to forward traffic to a member of an **Auto Scaling Groups**. Auto Scaling Groups are collections of EC2 instances that are treated as a logical group. ELB use health checks (TCP or HTTP) that help the load balancer determine whether to forward traffic to a particular EC2 instance.

In this recipe, we'll use the AWS CLI tool to create an Auto Scaling Groups and attach an ELB to it. We won't cover configuration management or deployment in this recipe, so imagine that you have a microservice running on each of the EC2 instances in the Auto Scaling Groups.

How to do it...

1. We'll be using the AWS CLI in this recipe, a command-line utility written in Python, that makes interacting with the AWS API easy. We'll assume you have an AWS account and have installed and configured the AWS CLI application. Consult the AWS documentation (https://docs.aws.amazon.com/cli/latest/index.html#) for installation instructions.

2. Create a launch configuration. Launch configurations are templates that our Auto Scaling Groups will use for creating new EC2 instances. They contain information such as the instance type and size that we want to use when creating new instances. Give your launch configuration a unique name–in our case, we'll simply call it `users-service-launch-configuration`:

```
$ aws create-launch-configuration --launch-configuration-name
users-service-launch-configuration \
   --image-id ami-05355a6c --security-groups sg-8422d1eb \
   --instance-type m3.medium
```

3. Create an Auto Scaling Groups that uses our new launch configuration:

```
$ aws create-auto-scaling-group --auto-scaling-group-name users-
service-asg \
   --launch-configuration-name users-service-launch-configuration \
   --min-size 2 \
   --max-size 10
```

4. Create an ELB, as follows:

```
$ aws create-load-balancer --load-balancer-name users-service-elb \
   --listeners
"Protocol=HTTP,LoadBalancerPort=80,InstanceProtocol=HTTP,InstancePo
rt=8080"
```

5. Attach the ASG to our load balancer by running the following command line:

```
$ aws autoscaling attach-load-balancers --auto-scaling-group-name
users-service-asg --load-balancer-names users-service-elb
```

Client-side load balancing

Server-side load balancing is a well-established and battle-tested way to distribute load to an application. It has drawbacks, however, in that there is an upper limit to the amount of incoming connections that a single load balancer can handle. This can be at least partially solved with round-robin DNS, which would distribute load to a number of load balancers, but this configuration can quickly become cumbersome and costly. Load balancer applications can also become points of failure in an already-complex microservices architecture.

An increasingly popular alternative to server-side load balancing is client-side load balancing. In this convention, clients are responsible for distributing requests evenly to running instances of a service. Clients can keep track of latency and failure rates from nodes and opt to reduce the amount of traffic to nodes that are experiencing high latency or high failure rates. This method of load balancing can be extremely effective and simple, especially in large-scale applications.

Ribbon is an open source library developed by Netflix that, among other features, provides support for client-side load balancing. In this recipe, we'll modify our message service to use `ribbon` for client-side load balancing. Instead of sending our requests for a user's friendships to a single instance of the users service, we'll distribute load to a number of available instances.

How to do it...

1. Open the `message-service` project and add the following lines to `build.gradle`:

```
...
dependencies {
  ...
  compile group: 'org.springframework.cloud', name: 'spring-cloud-
starter-ribbon', version: '1.4.2.RELEASE'
}
...
```

2. Navigate to `src/main/resources/application.yml` and add the following configuration for `users-service`:

```
users-service:
  ribbon:
    eureka:
      enabled: false
    listOfServers: localhost:8090,localhost:9092,localhost:9999
    ServerListRefreshInterval: 15000
```

3. Create a new Java class called `UsersServiceConfiguration`. This class will configure the specific rules we want `ribbon` to follow when deciding how to distribute load:

```java
package com.packtpub.microservices.ch03.clientsideloadbalancing;

import org.springframework.beans.factory.annotation.Autowired;
import org.springframework.context.annotation.Bean;

import com.netflix.client.config.IClientConfig;
import com.netflix.loadbalancer.IPing;
import com.netflix.loadbalancer.IRule;
import com.netflix.loadbalancer.PingUrl;
import com.netflix.loadbalancer.AvailabilityFilteringRule;

public class UsersServiceConfiguration {

  @Autowired
  IClientConfig ribbonClientConfig;

  @Bean
  public IPing ribbonPing(IClientConfig config) {
    return new PingUrl();
  }

  @Bean
  public IRule ribbonRule(IClientConfig config) {
    return new AvailabilityFilteringRule();
  }

}
```

4. Open `MessageController` and add the following annotation to the
`MessageController` class:

```
@RibbonClient(name = "users-service", configuration =
UsersServiceConfiguration.class)
@RestClient
public class MessageController {


}
```

5. Annotate the `RestTemplate` class to indicate that we want it to use `ribbon`
load-balancing support, and modify our URL to use the service name, not the
hostname we had hardcoded previously:

```
@RibbonClient(name = "users-service", configuration =
UsersServiceConfiguration.class)
@RestClient
public class MessageController {
    ...
    @LoadBalanced
    @Bean
    RestTemplate restTemplate(){
      return new RestTemplate();
    }
    ...

    @Async
    public CompletableFuture<Boolean> isFollowing(String fromUser,
String toUser) {

        String url = String.format(
"http://localhost:4567/followings?user=%s&filter=%s",
                fromUser, toUser);

        RestTemplate template = new RestTemplate();
        UserFriendships followings = template.getForObject(url,
UserFriendships.class);

        return CompletableFuture.completedFuture(
                followings.getFriendships().isEmpty()
        );
    }
}
```

Building event-driven microservices

So far, all of our service-to-service communication recipes have involved having one service call one or more other services directly. This is necessary when the response from the downstream service is required to fulfill the user's request. This isn't always required however. In cases when you want to react to an event in the system, for example, when you want to send an email or notification or when you want to update an analytics store, using an event-driven architecture is preferable. In this design, one service produces a message to a broker and another application consumes that message and performs an action. This has the benefit of decoupling the publisher from the consumer (so your message service doesn't have to worry about sending email notifications, for instance) and also removing potentially expensive operations off the critical path of the user's request. The event-driven architecture also provide some level of fault tolerance as consumers can fail, and messages can be replayed to retry any failed operations.

Apache Kafka is an open source stream-processing platform. At its core, it is an event broker architected as a distributed transaction log. A full description of Apache Kafka is worthy of an entire book in itself—for a great introduction, I highly recommend reading the LinkedIn blog post that introduces Kafka (`https://engineering.linkedin.com/distributed-systems/log-what-every-software-engineer-should-know-about-real-time-datas-unifying`). The minimum you need to know to follow this recipe is that Kafka is a distributed event store that lets you publish messages to categories called **topics**. Another process can then consume messages from a topic and react to them.

Going back to our fictional messaging application, when a user sends a message to another user, we want to be able to notify the recipient in a number of ways. Depending on the recipient's preferences, we'll probably send an email or a push notification or both. In this recipe, we'll modify our message service from previous recipes to publish an event to a Kafka topic called **messages**. We'll then build a consumer application that listens for events in the message's topic and can react by sending the recipient notifications.

How to do it...

Spring for Apache Kafka (`spring-kafka`) is a project that makes it easy to integrate Spring applications with Apache Kafka. It provides useful abstractions for sending and receiving messages.

Note that to follow the steps in this recipe, you will need to have a version of Kafka and ZooKeeper running and accessible. Installing and configuring these two pieces of software is beyond the scope of this recipe, so please visit the respective project websites and follow their wonderfully written guides on getting started. In this recipe, we'll assume that you have Kafka running a single broker on port 9092 and a single instance of ZooKeeper running on port 2181.

Message producer

1. Open the `message-service` project from previous recipes. Modify the `build.gradle` file and add the `spring-kafka` project to the list of dependencies:

```
dependencies {
    compile group: 'org.springframework.kafka', name: 'spring-kafka', version: '2.1.1.RELEASE'
    compile group: 'org.springframework.boot', name: 'spring-boot-starter-web'
    testCompile group: 'junit', name: 'junit', version: '4.12'
}
```

2. The `spring-kafka` project provides a template for sending messages to a Kafka broker. To use the template in our project, we'll need to create a `ProducerFactory` interface and provide it to the constructor of the template.

3. Open the `Application.java` file and add the following content. Note that we're hardcoding the network location of the Kafka broker here—in a real application, you'd at least place this value in some kind of configuration (preferably respecting 12 factor conventions):

```java
package com.packtpub.microservices.ch03.message;

import org.apache.kafka.clients.producer.ProducerConfig;
import org.apache.kafka.common.serialization.StringSerializer;
import org.springframework.boot.SpringApplication;
import org.springframework.boot.autoconfigure.SpringBootApplication;
import org.springframework.context.annotation.Bean;
import org.springframework.kafka.core.DefaultKafkaProducerFactory;
import org.springframework.kafka.core.KafkaTemplate;
import org.springframework.kafka.core.ProducerFactory;

import java.util.HashMap;
import java.util.Map;
```

```
@SpringBootApplication
@EnableAsync
public class Application {
    public static void main(String[] args) {
        SpringApplication.run(Application.class, args);
    }

    @Bean
    public Map<String, Object> producerConfigs() {
        Map<String, Object> props = new HashMap<>();
        props.put(ProducerConfig.BOOTSTRAP_SERVERS_CONFIG,
"localhost:9092");
        props.put(ProducerConfig.KEY_SERIALIZER_CLASS_CONFIG,
StringSerializer.class);
        props.put(ProducerConfig.VALUE_SERIALIZER_CLASS_CONFIG,
StringSerializer.class);
        return props;
    }

    @Bean
    public ProducerFactory<Integer, String> producerFactory() {
        return new
DefaultKafkaProducerFactory<>(producerConfigs());
    }

    @Bean
    public KafkaTemplate<Integer, String> kafkaTemplate() {
        return new KafkaTemplate<Integer,
String>(producerFactory());
    }
}
```

4. Now that we can use `KafkaTemplate` in our application, add one to the `MessageController` class. Also, use the Jackson `ObjectMapper` class to convert our `Message` instance into a JSON string that we'll publish to the Kafka topic. Open the `MessageController` class and add following fields:

```
...
import org.springframework.kafka.core.KafkaTemplate;
import com.fasterxml.jackson.databind.ObjectMapper;
...


@RestController
public class MessageController {

    @Autowired
```

```
      private KafkaTemplate kafkaTemplate;

      @Autowired
      private ObjectMapper objectMapper;

      ...
}
```

5. Now that we have access to the Jackson `ObjectMapper` and the `KafkaTemplate` classes, create a method for publishing events. In this example, we're printing out to standard error and standard output. In a real application, you'd configure a logger, such as log4j, and use the appropriate log levels:

```
@RestController
public class MessageController {

      ...

      private void publishMessageEvent(Message message) {
          try {
              String data = objectMapper.writeValueAsString(message);
              ListenableFuture<SendResult> result =
      kafkaTemplate.send("messages", data);
              result.addCallback(new
      ListenableFutureCallback<SendResult>() {
                  @Override
                  public void onFailure(Throwable ex) {
                      System.err.println("Failed to emit message
      event: " + ex.getMessage());
                  }

                  @Override
                  public void onSuccess(SendResult result) {
                      System.out.println("Successfully published
      message event");
                  }
              });
          } catch (JsonProcessingException e) {
              System.err.println("Error processing json: " +
      e.getMessage());
          }
      }
}
```

6. Add the following line to the `create` method, calling the previously created the `publishMessageEvent` method:

```
@RequestMapping(
            path="/messages",
            method=RequestMethod.POST,
            produces="application/json")
public ResponseEntity<Message> create(@RequestBody Message message)
{

    ...

    publishMessageEvent(message);
    return ResponseEntity.created(location).build();
}
```

7. To test this example, create a message topic using the `kafka-topics.sh` Kafka utility (packaged with the Kafka binary distribution), as follows:

```
bin/kafka-topics.sh --create \
  --zookeeper localhost:2181 \
  --replication-factor 1 --partitions 1 \
  --topic messages
```

Message consumer

Now that we're publishing message-send events, the next step is to build a small consumer application that can react to these events in our system. We'll discuss the scaffolding as it relates to Kafka in this recipe; implementing email and push notification functionality is left as an exercise for the reader:

1. Create a new Gradle Java project called `message-notifier` with the following `build.gradle` file:

```
group 'com.packtpub.microservices'
version '1.0-SNAPSHOT'

buildscript {
    repositories {
        mavenCentral()
    }
    dependencies {
        classpath group: 'org.springframework.boot', name: 'spring-
boot-gradle-plugin', version: '1.5.9.RELEASE'
    }
}
```

```
apply plugin: 'java'
apply plugin: 'org.springframework.boot'

sourceCompatibility = 1.8

repositories {
    mavenCentral()
}

dependencies {
    compile group: 'org.springframework.kafka', name: 'spring-
kafka', version: '2.1.1.RELEASE'
    compile group: 'org.springframework.boot', name: 'spring-boot-
starter'
    testCompile group: 'junit', name: 'junit', version: '4.12'
}
```

2. Create a new Java class called `Application` with the Spring Boot application boilerplate:

```
package com.packtpub.microservices.ch03.consumer;

import org.springframework.boot.SpringApplication;
import
org.springframework.boot.autoconfigure.SpringBootApplication;

@SpringBootApplication
public class Application {
    public static void main(String[] args) {
        SpringApplication.run(Application.class, args);
    }
}
```

Evolving APIs

APIs are contracts between clients and servers. Backward-incompatible changes to APIs can cause unexpected errors for clients of the service. In a microservices architecture, precautions have to be taken to ensure that changes to a service's API do not unintentionally cause cascading problems throughout the system.

A popular approach is to version your API, either through the URL or via content negotiation in request headers. Because they're generally easier to work with, and often easier to cache, URL prefixes or query strings tend to be more common—in this case, the API endpoint is either prefixed with a version string (that is, `/v1/users`) or called with a query string parameter specifying a version or even a date (that is, `/v1/users?version=1.0` or `/v1/users?version=20180122`).

With edge proxies or service mesh configurations, it's even possible to run multiple versions of software in an environment and route requests based on the URL to older or newer versions of a service. This changes the traditional life cycle of a service–you can safely decommission a version when it is no longer receiving any traffic. This can be useful, especially in the case of a public API where you have little control over clients.

Microservices are different than public APIs. The contract between clients and the server in a public API is much more long-lived. In a microservices architecture, it's easier to track down clients who are using your service and convince them to upgrade their code! Nevertheless, API versioning is sometimes necessary. Because being able to respond successfully to multiple versions of an API is a maintenance burden, we'd like to avoid it for as long as possible. To do this, there are a few practices that can be used to avoid making backward-incompatible changes.

How to do it...

1. Using our example application, `pichat`, let's imagine that we want to change the name of the message body from `body` to `message_text`. This presents a problem because our message service is designed to accept the following requests:

```
GET /messages?user_id=123
GET /messages/123
POST /messages
DELETE /messages/123
```

2. In the case of the GET requests, the client will expect a JSON object with a field called body in the response. In the case of the POST request, clients will be sending payloads as the JSON objects with a field called body. We can't simply remove body because that would break existing clients, thus necessitating a change to the API version. Instead, we'll simply add the new field in addition to the old one, as follows:

```
{
  "message": {
    "from_user": "sender",
    "to_user": "recipient",
    "body": "Hello, there",
    "message_text": "Hello, there"
  }
}
```

3. Now you can gradually track down clients using these responses; once they've all been upgraded, you can safely remove the deprecated field from the JSON response.

Client Patterns

4

In this chapter, we will cover the following recipes:

- Modeling concurrency with dependent futures
- Backend For Frontend
- Consistent RPC with HTTP and JSON
- Using gRPC
- Using Thrift

Introduction

When building a service-oriented architecture, it's easy to get stuck thinking about the most general way to represent the domain entities and behaviors that are controlled by a particular service. The truth is, we rarely use services in general ways—we usually combine calls to multiple services and use the responses to create a new, aggregate response body. We often make service calls in ways that resemble how we used to aggregate data from a database, so we have to think about relationships between disparate types in our system and how best to model data dependencies.

We also want to make client development easy. When designing general-purpose APIs, it's easy to get stuck thinking about the right way to do things (if you've ever heard someone critique an API design as not being RESTful, this might sound familiar) instead of thinking about the easy way to do things. A service isn't much good if a client needs to make dozens of calls to it in order to get the data they need. When designing systems that involve microservices, it's essential to think about data aggregation from the client's perspective.

Clients have to think about more than just the services they are invoking, but often they have to consider what instance of those services they want to configure themselves to invoke. It's common to have staging or testing environments, and these get much more complicated in the microservices architectures.

In this chapter, we'll discuss techniques for modeling dependent service calls and aggregating responses from various services to create client-specific APIs. We'll also discuss managing different microservices environments and making RPC consistent with JSON and HTTP, as well as the gRPC and Thrift binary protocols.

Modeling concurrency with dependent futures

We saw in a previous recipe that we can use asynchronous methods to make service calls that are handled in separate threads. This is essential because blocking on network I/O would severely limit the number of incoming requests our service would be able to handle. A service that blocks on the network I/O would only be able to handle a relatively small number of requests per process, requiring us to spend more resources on horizontal scaling. In the example we used, the message service needed to call the social graph service for two users, the sender, and the recipient of a message, and make sure that the two users followed each other before allowing a message to be sent. We modified our request methods to return the `CompletableFuture` instances that wrapped the response, and then waited on all of the results to finish before verifying that the sender and recipient of the message had a symmetric following relationship. This model works fine when you're making multiple requests that are not dependent (you do not need the response from one request to make the subsequent request). In this situation, where we have dependent service calls, we need a better way to model that dependency.

In our `pichat` application, we need to render a screen that lists information about users we follow. In order to do that, we need to call the social-graph service to get a list of users and then call the users service to get details such as the display name and avatar for each user. This use case involves making dependent service calls. We need an effective way of modeling this kind of service invocation while still scheduling asynchronous operations in ways that allow them to be run in separate threads of execution.

In this recipe, we'll demonstrate this by using composition of `CompletableFuture` as well as Java 8 streams to model dependent service invocations. We'll create a sample client application that calls a social service to get a list of users that the logged in user follows, and then calls the user service to get details for each user.

How to do it...

In order to model dependent asynchronous service calls, we'll take advantage of two features in Java 8. Streams are useful for processing data, so we'll use them in our example to extract usernames from a list of followings and map a function to each element. Java 8's `CompletableFuture` can be composed, which allows us to naturally express dependencies between futures.

In this recipe, we'll create a simple client application that calls the social service for a list of users that the current user follows. For each user returned, the application will get user details from the users service. We'll build this example as a command-line application for easy demonstration purposes, but it could just as well be another microservice, or a web or mobile client.

 In order to build a command-line application that has all of the capabilities of a Spring Boot application, we're going to cheat a little and just implement `CommandLineRunner` and call `System.exit(0);` in the `run()` method.

Before we start building our application, we'll outline the responses from our hypothetical social service and users service services. We can mimic these services by just hosting the appropriate JSON response on a local web server. We'll use ports `8000` and `8001` for the social service and users service, respectively. The social service has an endpoint, `/followings/:username`, that returns a JSON object with a list of followings for the specified username. The JSON response will look like the following snippet:

```
{
  "username": "paulosman",
  "followings": [
    "johnsmith",
    "janesmith",
    "petersmith"
  ]
}
```

The users service has an endpoint called `/users/:username`, which will return a JSON representation of the user's details, including the username, full name, and avatar URL:

```
{
  "username": "paulosman",
  "full_name": "Paul Osman",
  "avatar_url": "http://foo.com/pic.jpg"
}
```

Now that we have our services and we've outlined the responses we expect from each, let's go ahead and build our client application by performing the following steps:

1. Create a new Java/Gradle application called `UserDetailsClient` with the following `build.gradle` file:

```
group 'com.packtpub.microservices'
version '1.0-SNAPSHOT'

buildscript {
    repositories {
        mavenCentral()
    }
    dependencies {
        classpath group: 'org.springframework.boot', name: 'spring-
boot-gradle
        -plugin', version: '1.5.9.RELEASE'
    }
}

apply plugin: 'java'
apply plugin: 'org.springframework.boot'

sourceCompatibility = 1.8

repositories {
    mavenCentral()
}

dependencies {
    testCompile group: 'junit', name: 'junit', version: '4.12'
    compile group: 'org.springframework.boot',
    name: 'spring-boot-starter-web'
}
```

2. Create a package called `com.packtpub.microservices.ch04.user.models` and a new class called `UserDetails`. We'll use this class to model our response from the users service:

```
package com.packtpub.microservices.ch04.user.models;

import com.fasterxml.jackson.annotation.JsonProperty;

public class UserDetails {
    private String username;

    @JsonProperty("display_name")
```

```java
    private String displayName;

    @JsonProperty("avatar_url")
    private String avatarUrl;

    public UserDetails() {}

    public UserDetails(String username, String displayName,
    String avatarUrl) {
        this.username = username;
        this.displayName = displayName;
        this.avatarUrl = avatarUrl;
    }

    public String getUsername() {
        return username;
    }

    public void setUsername(String username) {
        this.username = username;
    }

    public String getDisplayName() {
        return displayName;
    }

    public void setDisplayName(String displayName) {
        this.displayName = displayName;
    }

    public String getAvatarUrl() {
        return avatarUrl;
    }

    public void setAvatarUrl(String avatarUrl) {
        this.avatarUrl = avatarUrl;
    }

    public String toString() {
        return String.format("[UserDetails: %s, %s, %s]", username,
        displayName, avatarUrl);
    }
}
```

3. Create another class in the
   `com.packtpub.microservices.ch04.user.models` package called
   `Followings`. This will be used to model the response from the social service:

```
package com.packtpub.microservices.ch04.user.models;

import java.util.List;

public class Followings {
    private String username;
    private List<String> followings;

    public Followings() {}

    public Followings(String username, List<String> followings) {
        this.username = username;
        this.followings = followings;
    }

    public String getUsername() {
        return username;
    }

    public void setUsername(String username) {
        this.username = username;
    }

    public List<String> getFollowings() {
        return followings;
    }

    public void setFollowings(List<String> followings) {
        this.followings = followings;
    }

    public String toString() {
        return String.format("[Followings for username: %s - %s]",
        username, followings);
    }
}
```

4. Create a service representation for calling our social service. Predictably enough, we'll call it `SocialService` and put it in the `com.packtpub.microservices.ch04.user.services` package:

```
package com.packtpub.microservices.ch04.user.services;

import com.packtpub.microservices.models.Followings;
import org.springframework.boot.web.client.RestTemplateBuilder;
import org.springframework.scheduling.annotation.Async;
import org.springframework.stereotype.Service;
import org.springframework.web.client.RestTemplate;

import java.util.concurrent.CompletableFuture;

@Service
public class SocialService {

    private final RestTemplate restTemplate;

    public SocialService(RestTemplateBuilder restTemplateBuilder) {
        this.restTemplate = restTemplateBuilder.build();
    }

    @Async
    public CompletableFuture<Followings>
    getFollowings(String username) {
        String url =
String.format("http://localhost:8000/followings/
%s", username);
        Followings followings = restTemplate.getForObject(url,
        Followings.class);
        return CompletableFuture.completedFuture(followings);
    }
}
```

5. Create a service representation for our users service. Appropriately, we'll call the class `UserService` in the same package:

```
package com.packtpub.microservices.services;

import com.packtpub.microservices.models.Followings;
import com.packtpub.microservices.models.UserDetails;
import org.springframework.boot.web.client.RestTemplateBuilder;
import org.springframework.scheduling.annotation.Async;
import org.springframework.stereotype.Service;
import org.springframework.web.client.RestTemplate;
```

```
import java.util.concurrent.CompletableFuture;

@Service
public class UserService {
    private final RestTemplate restTemplate;

    public UserService(RestTemplateBuilder restTemplateBuilder) {
        this.restTemplate = restTemplateBuilder.build();
    }

    @Async
    public CompletableFuture<UserDetails>
    getUserDetails(String username) {
        String url = String.format("http://localhost:8001/users/
        %s", username);
        UserDetails userDetails = restTemplate.getForObject(url,
        UserDetails.class);
        return CompletableFuture.completedFuture(userDetails);
    }
}
```

6. We now have classes to model the responses from our services, and service objects to represent the services we're going to invoke. It's time to tie it all together by creating our main class, which will call these two services in a dependent manner, using the composability of futures to model the dependency. Create a new class called UserDetailsClient, as follows:

```
package com.packtpub.microservices.ch04.user;

import com.packtpub.microservices.models.Followings;
import com.packtpub.microservices.models.UserDetails;
import com.packtpub.microservices.services.SocialService;
import com.packtpub.microservices.services.UserService;
import org.springframework.beans.factory.annotation.Autowired;
import org.springframework.boot.CommandLineRunner;
import org.springframework.boot.SpringApplication;
import
org.springframework.boot.autoconfigure.SpringBootApplication;

import java.util.List;
import java.util.concurrent.CompletableFuture;
import java.util.concurrent.Future;
import java.util.stream.Collectors;

@SpringBootApplication
public class UserDetailsClient implements CommandLineRunner {
```

```
public UserDetailsClient() {}

@Autowired
private SocialService socialService;

@Autowired
private UserService userService;

public CompletableFuture<List<UserDetails>>
getFollowingDetails(String username) {
    return socialService.getFollowings(username).thenApply(f ->
            f.getFollowings().stream().map(u ->userService.
            getUserDetails(u)).map(CompletableFuture::join).
            collect(Collectors.toList()));
}

public static void main(String[] args) {
    SpringApplication.run(UserDetailsClient.class, args);
}

@Override
public void run(String... args) throws Exception {
    Future<List<UserDetails>> users = getFollowingDetails
    ("paulosman");
    System.out.println(users.get());
    System.out.println("Heyo");
    System.exit(0);
}
}
```

The magic really happens in the following method:

```
CompletableFuture<List<UserDetails>> getFollowingDetails(String
username)
{
  return socialService.getFollowings(username).thenApply(
    f -> f.getFollowings().stream().map(u ->
      userService.getUserDetails(u)).map(
        CompletableFuture::join).collect(Collectors.toList()));
}
```

Recall that the `getFollowings` method in `SocialService` returns `CompletableFuture<Followings>`. `CompletableFuture` has a method, called `thenApply`, that takes the eventual result of the future (`Followings`) and applies it to be passed in the Lambda. In this case, we're taking `Followings` and using the Java 8 Stream API to call map on the list of usernames returned by the social service. The map applies each username to a function that calls `getUserDetails` on `UserService`. The `CompletableFuture::join` method is used to turn `List<Future<T>>` into `Future<List<T>>`, which is a common operation when performing these kinds of dependent service invocations. Finally, we collect the results and return them as a list.

Backend for frontend

When software shifted from desktop and web-based applications to mobile applications, distributed architectures became much more prevalent. It became a focus for many organizations to build a platform instead of just a product. This approach places a much larger emphasis on APIs that a product can expose to clients as well as third-party partners. As APIs became a given for any web-based application, it became popular to try to build client applications (mobile or JavaScript) on the same API used to provide functionality to the third-party partners. The idea is that if you exposed one well-designed, general-purpose API, you would have everything you need to build any kind of application. The general architecture looked like this:

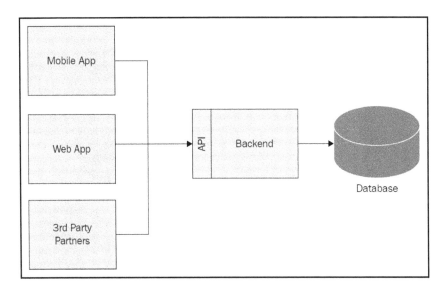

The flaw in this approach is that it assumes that the needs of your first-party (mobile and web) and third-party (partner) applications are always going to be aligned, and this is rarely the case. More often than not, you want to encourage certain kinds of functionality in the third-party integrations and a different set of functionality in first-party clients. Additionally, you want to be much more tolerant (encouraging, even) of changes in first-party clients—your client applications will evolve and constantly be changing their API requirements. Finally, you cannot anticipate all of the possible use cases third-party partners will have for your API, so a general-purpose design is beneficial, but you will be able to anticipate the needs of your mobile and web applications, and being too general in your API design can often hamper your product's needs. A good example of this is a server-side website that is rewritten as a single-page JavaScript application. With a general-purpose API, this kind of project can result in page views that require dozens of `XMLHttpRequests` to render a single page view.

Backend For Frontend (**BFF**) is an architectural pattern that involves creating separate, **bespoke APIs** for different classes of client applications. Instead of a single API layer in your architecture, separate BFF layers can be developed depending on how many categories of client applications you want to support. How you categorize clients is completely up to the needs of your business. You may decide to have a single BFF layer for all mobile clients, or you may divide them into an iOS BFF and an Android BFF. Similarly, you may choose to have a separate BFF layer for your web application and your third-party partners (what used to be the primary driver for your single API):

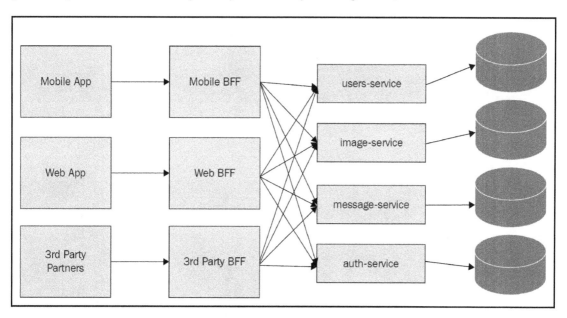

In this system, each category of client makes requests to its own BFF layer, which can then aggregate calls to downstream services and build a cohesive, bespoke API.

How to do it...

In order to design and build a BFF layer, we should first design the API. In fact, we've already done this. In the previous recipe, we demonstrated using `CompletableFuture` to asynchronously make a request to our systems, social service and then for each user returned, make asynchronous requests to the user-details-service to fetch certain user profile information. This is a great use case for a BFF layer for our mobile apps. Imagine that our mobile app has a screen that shows a list of users that the user follows, with basic information such as their avatar, username, and display name. Since the social graph information (the list of users the user is following) and the user profile information (avatar, username, and display name) are the responsibility of two separate services, it's cumbersome to require our mobile clients to aggregate calls to these services to render a following page. Instead, we can create a mobile BFF layer that handles this aggregation and returns a convenient response to the client. Our request endpoint would be as follows:

```
GET /users/:user_id/following
```

And the response body we expect to get back should be as follows:

```
{
  "username": "paulosman",
  "followings": [
    {
      "username": "friendlyuser",
      "display_name": "Friendly User",
      "avatar_url": "http://example.com/pic.jpg"
    },
    {
      ...
    }
  ]
}
```

As we can see, the BFF will return a response with all of the information we need to render a following screen in our mobile app:

1. Create a new Gradle/Java project called `bff-mobile` with the following `build.gradle` file:

```
group 'com.packtpub.microservices'
version '1.0-SNAPSHOT'

buildscript {
    repositories {
        mavenCentral()
    }
    dependencies {
        classpath group: 'org.springframework.boot',
        name: 'spring-boot-gradle-plugin',
        version: '1.5.9.RELEASE'
    }
}

apply plugin: 'java'
apply plugin: 'org.springframework.boot'

sourceCompatibility = 1.8

repositories {
    mavenCentral()
}

dependencies {
    testCompile group: 'junit', name: 'junit', version: '4.12'
    compile group: 'org.springframework.boot',
    name: 'spring-boot-starter-web'
}
```

2. Create a new package called `com.packtpub.microservices.mobilebff` and a new class called `Main`:

```
package com.packtpub.microservices.ch04.mobilebff;

import org.springframework.boot.SpringApplication;
import org.springframework.boot.autoconfigure.SpringBootApplication;

@SpringBootApplication
public class Main {
    public static void main(String[] args) {
```

```
                    SpringApplication.run(Main.class, args);
            }
        }
```

3. Create a new package called
   com.packtpub.microservices.ch04.mobilebff.models and a new class
   called User:

```
package com.packtpub.microservices.ch04.mobilebff.models;

import com.fasterxml.jackson.annotation.JsonProperty;

public class User {
    private String username;

    @JsonProperty("display_name")
    private String displayName;

    @JsonProperty("avatar_url")
    private String avatarUrl;

    public User() {}

    public User(String username, String displayName,
    String avatarUrl) {
        this.username = username;
        this.displayName = displayName;
        this.avatarUrl = avatarUrl;
    }

    public String getUsername() {
        return username;
    }

    public void setUsername(String username) {
        this.username = username;
    }

    public String getDisplayName() {
        return displayName;
    }

    public void setDisplayName(String displayName) {
        this.displayName = displayName;
    }

    public String getAvatarUrl() {
        return avatarUrl;
```

```
        }

        public void setAvatarUrl(String avatarUrl) {
            this.avatarUrl = avatarUrl;
        }

        public String toString() {
            return String.format(
                    "[User username:%s, displayName:%s, avatarUrl:%s]",
                    username, displayName, avatarUrl);
        }
    }
```

4. Create another model, called Followings:

```
    package com.packtpub.microservices.ch04.mobilebff.models;

    import java.util.List;

    public class Followings {
        private String username;

        private List<String> followings;

        public Followings() {}

        public Followings(String username, List<String> followings) {
            this.username = username;
            this.followings = followings;
        }

        public String getUsername() {
            return username;
        }

        public void setUsername(String username) {
            this.username = username;
        }

        public List<String> getFollowings() {
            return followings;
        }

        public void setFollowings(List<String> followings) {
            this.followings = followings;
        }
    }
```

5. The last model we'll create is called `HydratedFollowings`. This is similar to the `Followings` model, but instead of storing the list of users as a string, it contains a list of the `User` objects:

```
package com.packtpub.microservices.ch04.mobilebff.models;

import java.util.List;

public class HydratedFollowings {
    private String username;

    private List<User> followings;

    public HydratedFollowings() {}

    public HydratedFollowings(String username, List<User>
    followings) {
        this.username = username;
        this.followings = followings;
    }

    public String getUsername() {
        return username;
    }

    public void setUsername(String username) {
        this.username = username;
    }

    public List<User> getFollowings() {
        return followings;
    }

    public void setFollowings(List<User> followings) {
        this.followings = followings;
    }
}
```

6. Create the service clients. Create a new package called `com.packtpub.microservices.ch04.mobilebff.services` and a new class called `SocialGraphService`:

```
package com.packtpub.microservices.ch04.mobilebff.services;

import com.packtpub.microservices.ch04.mobilebff.models.Followings;
import org.springframework.boot.web.client.RestTemplateBuilder;
import org.springframework.scheduling.annotation.Async;
```

```
import org.springframework.stereotype.Service;
import org.springframework.web.client.RestTemplate;

import java.util.concurrent.CompletableFuture;

@Service
public class SocialGraphService {

    private final RestTemplate restTemplate;

    public SocialGraphService(RestTemplateBuilder
    restTemplateBuilder) {
        this.restTemplate = restTemplateBuilder.build();
    }

    @Async
    public CompletableFuture<Followings>
    getFollowing(String username) {
        String url =
String.format("http://localhost:4567/followings/
        %s", username);
        Followings followings = restTemplate.getForObject(url,
        Followings.class);
        return CompletableFuture.completedFuture(followings);
    }
}
```

7. Create a new class, called `UsersService`, that will serve as a client for our users service:

```
package com.packtpub.microservices.ch04.mobilebff.services;

import com.packtpub.microservices.ch04.mobilebff.models.User;
import org.springframework.boot.web.client.RestTemplateBuilder;
import org.springframework.scheduling.annotation.Async;
import org.springframework.stereotype.Service;
import org.springframework.web.client.RestTemplate;

import java.util.concurrent.CompletableFuture;

@Service
public class UsersService {

    private final RestTemplate restTemplate;

    public UsersService(RestTemplateBuilder restTemplateBuilder) {
        this.restTemplate = restTemplateBuilder.build();
    }
```

```
    @Async
    public CompletableFuture<User> getUserDetails(String username)
{
        String url = String.format("http://localhost:4568/users/
        %s", username);
        User user = restTemplate.getForObject(url, User.class);
        return CompletableFuture.completedFuture(user);
    }
}
```

8. Let's tie it all together by creating our controller that exposes the endpoint. This code will look familiar if you completed the previous recipe, since we're using exactly the same pattern to model dependent asynchronous service invocations. Create a package called `com.packtpub.microservices.ch04.mobilebff.controllers` and a new class called `UsersController`:

```
package com.packtpub.microservices.ch04.mobilebff.controllers;

import
com.packtpub.microservices.ch04.mobilebff.models.HydratedFollowings
;
import com.packtpub.microservices.ch04.mobilebff.models.User;
import
com.packtpub.microservices.ch04.mobilebff.services.SocialGraphServi
ce;
import
com.packtpub.microservices.ch04.mobilebff.services.UsersService;
import org.springframework.beans.factory.annotation.Autowired;
import org.springframework.web.bind.annotation.*;

import java.util.List;
import java.util.concurrent.CompletableFuture;
import java.util.concurrent.ExecutionException;
import java.util.stream.Collectors;

@RestController
public class UsersController {

    @Autowired
    private SocialGraphService socialGraphService;

    @Autowired
    private UsersService userService;

    @RequestMapping(path = "/users/{username}/followings",
    method = RequestMethod.GET)
```

```
      public HydratedFollowings getFollowings(@PathVariable String
username)
      throws ExecutionException, InterruptedException {
          CompletableFuture<List<User>> users =
socialGraphService.getFollowing
          (username).thenApply(f -> f.getFollowings().stream().map(
                         u -> userService.getUserDetails(u)).map(
CompletableFuture::join).collect(Collectors.toList()));
          return new HydratedFollowings(username, users.get());
      }
  }
```

9. That's it! Run the application and make a `GET` request to
   `/users/username/followings`. You should get back a fully-hydrated JSON
   response with the user's username and details for each of the users the user
   follows.

Consistent RPC with HTTP and JSON

When building multiple microservices, consistency and conventions between services start
to make a real impact. When problems arise in a microservice architecture, you can end up
spending time debugging many services—being able to make certain assumptions about
the nature of a particular service interface can save a lot of time and mental energy. Having
a consistent way of doing RPC also allows you to codify certain concerns into libraries that
can be easily shared between services. Things such as authentication, how headers should
be interpreted, what information is included in a response body, and how to request
paginated responses can be made simpler by having a consistent approach. Additionally,
the way that errors are reported should be made as consistent as possible.

Because the microservice architectures commonly consist of services written in different
programming languages by different teams, any efforts toward consistent RPC semantics
will have to be implemented, probably as libraries, in as many languages as you have used
to build services. This can be cumbersome, but is well worth the effort for the consistency
clients can assume when speaking to a variety of services.

In this recipe, we'll focus on services written in Java using Spring Boot. We'll write a custom
serializer to present resources and collections of resources in a consistent manner, including
pagination information. We'll then modify our message service to use our new serializer.

How to do it...

In this recipe, we'll create a wrapper class to represent collections of resources with pagination information. We'll also use the `JsonRootName` annotation from the `jackson` library to make single-resource representations consistent. The following code should be added to the message service, which was introduced in a previous recipe:

1. Create a new class called `ResourceCollection`. This class will be a regular POJO with fields to represent the page number, a list of items, and a URL that can be used to access the next page in a collection:

```
package com.packtpub.microservices.ch04.message.models;

import com.fasterxml.jackson.annotation.JsonProperty;
import com.fasterxml.jackson.annotation.JsonRootName;

import java.util.List;

@JsonRootName("result")
public class ResourceCollection<T> {

    private int page;

    @JsonProperty("next_url")
    private String nextUrl;

    private List<T> items;

    public ResourceCollection(List<T> items, int page, String
nextUrl) {
        this.items = items;
        this.page = page;
        this.nextUrl = nextUrl;
    }

    public int getPage() {
        return page;
    }

    public void setPage(int pageNumber) {
        this.page = page;
    }

    public String getNextUrl() {
        return nextUrl;
    }
```

```java
    public void setNextUrl(String nextUrl) {
        this.nextUrl = nextUrl;
    }

    public List<T> getItems() {
        return items;
    }

    public void setItems(List<T> items) {
        this.items = items;
    }
}
```

2. Create or modify the `Message` model. We're using the `JsonRootName` annotation here to wrap the `Message` representation in a single JSON object with the `item` key. In order to have consistent representations, we should add these to all models that our services expose as a resource:

```java
package com.packtpub.microservices.ch04.message.models;

import com.fasterxml.jackson.annotation.JsonRootName;

@JsonRootName("item")
public class Message {
    private String id;
    private String toUser;
    private String fromUser;
    private String body;

    public Message(String id, String toUser, String fromUser,
String body) {
        this.id = id;
        this.toUser = toUser;
        this.fromUser = fromUser;
        this.body = body;
    }

    public String getId() {
        return id;
    }

    public void setId(String id) {
        this.id = id;
    }

    public String getToUser() {
        return toUser;
```

```
        }

        public void setToUser(String toUser) {
            this.toUser = toUser;
        }

        public String getFromUser() {
            return fromUser;
        }

        public void setFromUser(String fromUser) {
            this.fromUser = fromUser;
        }

        public String getBody() {
            return body;
        }

        public void setBody(String body) {
            this.body = body;
        }
    }
```

3. The following controller returns a list of messages and a specific message. We wrap the list of messages in the `ResourceCollection` class that we created previously:

```
package com.packtpub.microservices.ch04.message.controllers;

import com.packtpub.microservices.ch04.message.models.Message;
import
com.packtpub.microservices.ch04.message.models.ResourceCollection;
import org.springframework.web.bind.annotation.*;

import javax.servlet.http.HttpServletRequest;
import java.util.List;
import java.util.stream.Collectors;
import java.util.stream.Stream;

@RestController
public class MessageController {

    @RequestMapping(value = "/messages", method =
RequestMethod.GET)
    public ResourceCollection<Message>
messages(@RequestParam(name="page", required=false,
defaultValue="1") int page,
                                        HttpServletRequest request)
```

```
{
        List<Message> messages = Stream.of(
                new Message("1234","paul", "veronica", "hello!"),
                new Message("5678","meghann", "paul", "hello!")
        ).collect(Collectors.toList());

        String nextUrl = String.format("%s?page=%d",
request.getRequestURI(), page + 1);

        return new ResourceCollection<>(messages, page, nextUrl);
    }

    @RequestMapping(value = "/messages/{id}", method =
RequestMethod.GET)
    public Message message(@PathVariable("id") String id) {
        return new Message(id, "paul", "veronica", "hi dad");
    }
}
```

4. If you test requesting a collection of items by making a request to /messages, the following JSON should now be returned:

```
{
    "result": {
        "page": 1,
        "items": [
            {
                "id": "1234",
                "toUser": "paul",
                "fromUser": "veronica",
                "body": "hello!"
            },
            {
                "id": "5678",
                "toUser": "meghann",
                "fromUser": "paul",
                "body": "hello!"
            }
        ],
        "next_url": "/messages?page=2"
    }
}
```

5. The following JSON should be returned for a single resource:

```
{
    "item": {
        "id": "123",
        "toUser": "paul",
        "fromUser": "veronica",
        "body": "hi dad"
    }
}
```

Having some standardization for how resources or lists of resources are represented can greatly simplify working with services in a microservices architecture. Doing this with JSON and HTTP involves a fair amount of manual work however, which can be abstracted away. In the next recipes, we'll explore using Thrift and gRPC, two alternatives to HTTP/JSON for RPC.

Using Thrift

JSON and HTTP are simple, straightforward solutions for data transportation and definition that should serve the purposes of many microservice architectures. If you want type safety and often better performance, however, it can be worthwhile to look at binary solutions such as Thrift or gRPC.

Apache Thrift is an **interface definition language** (**IDL**) and binary transport protocol invented at Facebook. It allows you to specify APIs by defining the structs (which are similar to objects in most languages) and exceptions that your service exposes. Thrift interfaces defined in the IDL are used to generate code in a supported language that is then used to manage the RPC calls. Supported languages include C, C++, Python, Ruby, and Java.

The benefits of a binary protocol such as Thrift are primarily improved performance and type safety. Depending on the JSON library used, serializing and deserializing large JSON payloads can be quite expensive and JSON does not have any type system that clients can use when handling responses. Additionally, because Thrift includes an IDL that can be used to generate code in any supported language, it's easy to let Thrift handle the generation of both client and server code, cutting down the amount of manual work needing to be done.

Because Apache Thrift doesn't use HTTP as the transport layer, services that export Thrift interfaces start their own Thrift server. In this recipe, we'll define the IDL for our message service and use Thrift to generate the handler code. We'll then create the server boilerplate that handles starting the service, listening on a specified port, and so on.

How to do it...

1. Create a new Gradle/Java project with the following `build.gradle` file:

```
group 'com.packtpub.microservices'
version '1.0-SNAPSHOT'

buildscript {
    repositories {
        maven {
            url "https://plugins.gradle.org/m2/"
        }
    }
    dependencies {
        classpath "gradle.plugin.org.jruyi.gradle:thrift-gradle-plugin:0.4.0"
    }
}

apply plugin: 'java'
apply plugin: 'org.jruyi.thrift'
apply plugin: 'application'

mainClassName =
'com.packtpub.microservices.ch04.MessageServiceServer'

compileThrift {
    recurse true

    generator 'html'
    generator 'java', 'private-members'
}

sourceCompatibility = 1.8

repositories {
    mavenCentral()
}

dependencies {
```

```
        compile group: 'org.apache.thrift', name: 'libthrift', version:
    '0.11.0'
        testCompile group: 'junit', name: 'junit', version: '4.12'
    }
```

2. Create a directory called `src/main/thrift` and a file called `service.thrift`. This is the IDL file for our service. We'll define a `MessageException` exception, the actual `Message` object, and a `MessageService` interface. For more information on the specific syntax of Thrift IDL files, the Thrift project website has good documentation (`https://thrift.apache.org/docs/idl`). To keep things simple, we'll just define a single method in our service that returns a list of messages for a specific user:

```
namespace java com.packtpub.microservices.ch04.thrift

exception MessageException {
    1: i32 code,
    2: string description
}

struct Message {
    1: i32 id,
    2: string from_user,
    3: string to_user,
    4: string body
}

service MessageService {
    list<Message> inbox(1: string username) throws
(1:MessageException e)
}
```

3. Running the assembled Gradle task will generate the code for the preceding IDL. We'll now create the implementation of our `MessageService` class. This will extend the autogenerated interface from the preceding IDL. For simplicity's sake, our `MessageService` implementation will not connect to any database but instead will use a static, hardcoded representation of inboxes that will be built in the constructor:

```
package com.packtpub.microservices.ch04.thrift;

import com.packtpub.microservices.ch04.thrift.Message;
import com.packtpub.microservices.ch04.thrift.MessageException;
import com.packtpub.microservices.ch04.thrift.MessageService;
import org.apache.thrift.TException;
```

```java
import java.util.HashMap;
import java.util.List;
import java.util.Map;
import java.util.stream.Collectors;
import java.util.stream.Stream;

public class MessageServiceImpl implements MessageService.Iface {

    private Map<String, List<Message>> messagesRepository;

    MessageServiceImpl() {
        // populate our mock repository with some sample messages
        messagesRepository = new HashMap<>();
        messagesRepository.put("usertwo", Stream.of(
            new Message(1234, "userone", "usertwo", "hi"),
            new Message(5678, "userthree", "usertwo", "hi")
        ).collect(Collectors.toList()));
        messagesRepository.put("userone", Stream.of(
            new Message(1122, "usertwo", "userone", "hi"),
            new Message(2233, "userthree", "userone", "hi")
        ).collect(Collectors.toList()));
    }

    @Override
    public List<Message> inbox(String username) throws TException {
        if (!messagesRepository.containsKey(username))
            throw new MessageException(100, "Inbox is empty");
        return messagesRepository.get(username);
    }
}
```

4. **Create the server.** Create a new class called `MessageServiceServer`, as follows:

```java
package com.packtpub.microservices.ch04.thrift;

import com.packtpub.microservices.ch04.thrift.MessageService;
import org.apache.thrift.server.TServer;
import org.apache.thrift.server.TSimpleServer;
import org.apache.thrift.transport.TServerSocket;
import org.apache.thrift.transport.TServerTransport;
import org.apache.thrift.transport.TTransportException;

public class MessageServiceServer {

    private TSimpleServer server;

    private void start() throws TTransportException {
```

```
        TServerTransport serverTransport = new TServerSocket(9999);
        server = new TSimpleServer(new
TServer.Args(serverTransport)
                .processor(new MessageService.Processor<>(new
MessageServiceImpl())));
        server.serve();
    }

    private void stop() {
        if (server != null && server.isServing())
            server.stop();
    }

    public static void main(String[] args) {
        MessageServiceServer service = new MessageServiceServer();
        try {
            if (args[1].equals("start"))
                service.start();
            else if (args[2].equals("stop"))
                service.stop();
        } catch (TTransportException e) {
            e.printStackTrace();
        }
    }
}
```

Your service is now built and uses Apache Thrift for RPC. As a further exercise, you can experiment with using the same IDL to generate client code that can be used to call this service.

Using gRPC

gRPC is an RPC framework originally invented at Google. Unlike Thrift, gRPC makes use of existing technologies, specifically **protocol buffers**, for its IDL and HTTP/2 for its transport layer. After having completed the previous recipe, aspects of gRPC will feel similar to aspects of Thrift. Instead of the Thrift IDL, types and services are defined in a .proto file. The .proto file can then be used to generate code using the protocol buffer's compiler.

How to do it...

1. Create a new Gradle/Java project with the following build.gradle file. Of note here is that we're installing and configuring the protobuf Gradle plugin, which will allow us to generate code from protobuf files using Gradle, and we're listing the required protobuf libraries as dependencies. Finally, we have to tell our IDE where to look for generated classes:

```gradle
group 'com.packtpub.microservices'
version '1.0-SNAPSHOT'

buildscript {
    repositories {
        mavenCentral()
    }
    dependencies {
        classpath 'com.google.protobuf:protobuf-gradle-
plugin:0.8.3'
    }
}

apply plugin: 'java'
apply plugin: 'com.google.protobuf'
apply plugin: 'application'

mainClassName =
'com.packtpub.microservices.ch04.grpc.MessageServer'

sourceCompatibility = 1.8

repositories {
    mavenCentral()
}

def grpcVersion = '1.10.0'

dependencies {
    compile group: 'com.google.api.grpc', name: 'proto-google-
common-protos', version: '1.0.0'
    compile group: 'io.grpc', name: 'grpc-netty', version:
grpcVersion
    compile group: 'io.grpc', name: 'grpc-protobuf', version:
grpcVersion
    compile group: 'io.grpc', name: 'grpc-stub', version:
grpcVersion
    testCompile group: 'junit', name: 'junit', version: '4.12'
```

```
    }

protobuf {
    protoc {
        artifact = 'com.google.protobuf:protoc:3.5.1-1'
    }
    plugins {
        grpc {
            artifact = "io.grpc:protoc-gen-grpc-
java:${grpcVersion}"
        }
    }
    generateProtoTasks {
        all()*.plugins {
            grpc {}
        }
    }
}

// Inform IDEs like IntelliJ IDEA, Eclipse or NetBeans about the
generated code.
sourceSets {
    main {
        java {
            srcDirs 'build/generated/source/proto/main/grpc'
            srcDirs 'build/generated/source/proto/main/java'
        }
    }
}
```

2. Create a new directory called `src/main/proto` and a new file called `message_service.proto`. This will be our definition of `protobuf` for our service. Like in the last recipe, we'll keep it simple by only exposing one method that returns a list of messages for a specified user:

```
option java_package = "com.packtpub.microservices.ch04.grpc";

message Username {
    required string username = 1;
}

message Message {
    required string id = 1;
    required string from_user = 2;
    required string to_user = 3;
    required string body = 4;
}
```

```
message InboxReply {
    repeated Message messages = 1;
}

service MessageService {
    rpc inbox(Username) returns (InboxReply) {}
}
```

3. Implement the actual service. In order to do this, we need to create a new class called `MessageServer` with all the necessary boilerplate for starting and stopping our server. We'll also create an inner class called `MessageService` that extends the generated `MessageServiceGrpc.MessageServiceImplBase` class:

```java
package com.packtpub.microservices.ch04.grpc;

import io.grpc.Server;
import io.grpc.ServerBuilder;
import io.grpc.stub.StreamObserver;

import java.io.IOException;

public class MessageServer {

    private final int port;
    private final Server server;

    private MessageServer(int port) throws IOException {
        this(ServerBuilder.forPort(port), port);
    }

    private MessageServer(ServerBuilder<?> serverBuilder, int port)
    {
        this.port = port;
        this.server = serverBuilder.addService(new
MessageService()).build();
    }

    public void start() throws IOException {
        server.start();
        Runtime.getRuntime().addShutdownHook(new Thread() {
            @Override
            public void run() {
                // Use stderr here since the logger may has been
reset by its JVM shutdown hook.
                System.err.println("*** shutting down gRPC server
since JVM is shutting down");
                MessageServer.this.stop();
```

```
                    System.err.println("*** server shut down");
            }
        });
    }

    public void stop() {
        if (server != null) {
            server.shutdown();
        }
    }

    private void blockUntilShutdown() throws InterruptedException {
        if (server != null) {
            server.awaitTermination();
        }
    }

    private static class MessageService extends
MessageServiceGrpc.MessageServiceImplBase {
        public void inbox(MessageServiceOuterClass.Username
request,
StreamObserver<MessageServiceOuterClass.InboxReply>
responseObserver) {
            MessageServiceOuterClass.InboxReply reply =
MessageServiceOuterClass.InboxReply.newBuilder().addMessages(
                MessageServiceOuterClass.Message.newBuilder()
                    .setId("1234")
                    .setFromUser("Paul")
                    .setToUser("Veronica")
                    .setBody("hi")
            ).addMessages(
                MessageServiceOuterClass.Message.newBuilder()
                    .setId("5678")
                    .setFromUser("FooBarUser")
                    .setToUser("Veronica")
                    .setBody("Hello again")
            ).build();
            responseObserver.onNext(reply);
            responseObserver.onCompleted();
        }
    }

    public static void main(String[] args) throws Exception {
        MessageServer server = new MessageServer(8989);
        server.start();
        server.blockUntilShutdown();
    }
}
```

Reliability Patterns

5

In this chapter, we will cover the following recipes:

- Using circuit breakers to implement backpressure
- Retrying requests with exponential backoff
- Improving performance with caching
- Fronting your services with a CDN
- Gracefully degrading the user experience
- Testing your failure scenarios with controlled game days
- Introducing automated chaos

Introduction

Reliability is becoming an increasingly popular topic in the world of distributed systems. Job postings for **Site Reliability Engineers** (**SRE**) or **chaos engineers** are becoming common, and as more and more organizations move toward cloud-native technologies, it's becoming impossible to ignore that system failure is always a reality. Networks will experience congestion, switches, other hardware components will fail, and a whole host of potential failure modes in systems will surprise us in production. It is impossible to completely prevent failures, so we should try to design our systems to be as tolerant of failure as possible.

Microservices provide interesting and useful opportunities to design for reliability. Because microservices encourage us to break our systems into services encapsulating single responsibilities, we can use a number of useful reliability patterns to isolate failures when they do occur. Microservice architectures also present a number of challenges when planning for reliability. Increased reliance on network requests, heterogeneous configurations, multiple data stores and connection pools, and different technical stacks all contribute to an inherently more complex environment where different styles of failure modes can surface.

Whether dealing with a microservice architecture or a monolith code base, we all find ourselves fundamentally surprised [1] (you can check this link for more information: `https://www.youtube.com/watch?v=tZ2wj2px06Q`) by the behavior of a system under some kind of failure state at one point or another. Building resiliency into our systems from the start allows us to optimize how we react in these situations. In this chapter, we'll discuss a number of useful reliability patterns that can be used when designing and building microservices to prepare for and reduce the impact of system failures, both expected and unexpected.

Using circuit breakers

Failures in distributed systems can be difficult to debug. A symptom (spikes in latency or a high error rate) can appear far away from the underlying cause (slow database query, garbage collection cycles causing a service to slow down the processing of requests). Sometimes a complete outage can be the result of a failure in a small part of the system, especially when components of the system are having difficulty handling increases in load.

Whenever possible, we want to prevent failures in one part of a system from cascading to other parts, causing widespread and hard-to-debug production issues. Furthermore, if a failure is temporary, we'd like our system to be able to self-repair when the failure is over. If a specific service is experiencing problems because of a temporary spike in load, we should design our system in such a way that it prevents requests to the unhealthy service, allowing it time to recover before beginning to send it traffic again.

Circuit breakers are used in houses to prevent the overuse of electricity from heating up the internal wiring and burning the house down. A circuit is tripped if the breaker detects that it is being overused and cannot handle the amount of current being drawn from it. After some time passes, the circuit can be closed again, allowing the system to function normally.

This same approach can be translated to software and applied to microservice architectures. When a service invokes another service, we should wrap the RPC call in a circuit breaker. If the request fails repeatedly, indicating that the service is unhealthy, the circuit breaker is opened, preventing any further requests from being attempted. The invoking service can then "fail fast" and decide how to handle the failure mode. After a configurable period of time, we can allow another request through, and if it succeeds, close the circuit again, allowing the system to resume normal operation. You can a look at the following related flowchart:

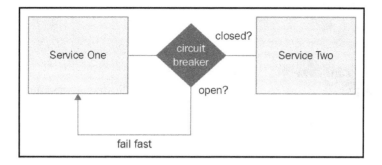

Libraries that implement circuit breakers are available for most popular programming languages. The Hystrix fault-tolerance library, built by Netflix and used in previous recipes is one such library. Some frameworks, such as Twitter's Finagle, automatically wrap RPCs in circuit breakers, keeping track of failures and automatically managing the state of the breaker. Open source service-mesh software, such as **Conduit** and **Linkerd**, automatically add circuit breakers to RPCs as well. In this recipe, we'll introduce a library called resilience4j and use its circuit breaker implementation to allow calls from one service to another to fail fast in the event of a failure threshold being reached. To make the example more concrete, we'll modify a message service, which calls a socialgraph service to determine whether two users follow each other, and wrap RPC calls in a circuit breaker.

How to do it...

To demonstrate wrapping service invocations in circuit breakers, we're going to create a version of the pichat message service that exposes endpoints for sending and retrieving messages. To send a message from a sender to a recipient, those two users must have a friendship. Friendships are handled by a social-graph-service. For the sake of simplicity, we'll code up a simple mock social-graph-service in Ruby, as we have done in previous recipes. The mock service will expose a single endpoint that lists friendships for a specified user. Here is the source code for the mock social-graph-service in Ruby:

```ruby
require 'sinatra'
require 'json'

get '/friendships/:username' do
  content_type :json
  {
    'username': params[:username],
    'friendships': [
      'pichat:users:johndoe',
      'pichat:users:janesmith',
      'pichat:users:anotheruser'
```

```
    ]
  }.to_json
end
```

 In our mock service, we're using strings in
the `pichat:users:username` format to identify users in our system.
These are pseudo-URIs, which uniquely identify users in our system. For
now, just know that these are unique strings used to identify users in our
system.

Our mock social-graph-service exposes the following single endpoint:

```
GET /friendships/paulosman
```

The preceding endpoint returns a JSON response body representing the friendships that the
requested user has:

```
{
  "username": "fdsa",
  "friendships": [
    "pichat:users:foobar",
    "pichat:users:asomefdsa"
  ]
}
```

With our mock social-graph-service running on the localhost, port `4567` (the default port
for Ruby Sinatra applications), we're ready to start writing our message service. As in
previous recipes, we'll use Java and the Spring Boot framework. We'll also use the
`resilience4j` circuit-breaker library to wrap calls from the message service to the social-
graph-service. First, we'll develop our message-service code, then we'll add in the
`resilience4j` circuit-breaker library to add a level of resilience to our service, as shown in
the following steps:

1. Create a new Gradle Java project and add the following code to `build.gradle`:

```
group 'com.packtpub.microservices'
version '1.0-SNAPSHOT'

buildscript {
    repositories {
        mavenCentral()
    }
    dependencies {
        classpath group: 'org.springframework.boot', name: 'spring-
boot-gradle-plugin', version: '1.5.9.RELEASE'
    }
```

```
}

apply plugin: 'java'
apply plugin: 'org.springframework.boot'

sourceCompatibility = 1.8

repositories {
    mavenCentral()
}

dependencies {
    testCompile group: 'junit', name: 'junit', version: '4.12'
    compile group: 'org.springframework.boot', name: 'spring-boot-
starter-web'
}
```

2. Our message-service code will have two beans that get autowired into our controller. The first is an in-memory message repository (in a real-world example, this would be replaced with a more durable persistence layer), and the second is a client for the social-graph-service. Before we create those, let's create some supporting objects. Create a new package called com.packtpub.microservices.ch05.message.exceptions and a new class called MessageNotFoundException. This will be used to indicate that a message cannot be found, which will result in a 404 response from our service, as shown here:

```
package com.packtpub.microservices.ch05.exceptions;

import org.springframework.http.HttpStatus;
import org.springframework.web.bind.annotation.ResponseStatus;

@ResponseStatus(HttpStatus.NOT_FOUND)
public class MessageNotFoundException extends Exception {
    public MessageNotFoundException(String message) {
super(message); }
}
```

3. Create another class in the exceptions package called MessageSendForbiddenException. This will be used to indicate that a message cannot be sent because the sender and the recipient are not friends. The response code from our service will be 403 forbidden, as shown here:

```
package com.packtpub.microservices.ch05.message.exceptions;

import org.springframework.http.HttpStatus;
```

```
import org.springframework.web.bind.annotation.ResponseStatus;

@ResponseStatus(HttpStatus.FORBIDDEN)
public class MessageSendForbiddenException extends Exception {
    public MessageSendForbiddenException(String message) {
super(message); }
}
```

4. Create the `SocialGraphClient` class. Create a new package called `com.packtpub.microservices.ch05.message.clients` and a new class called `SocialGraphClient`, as shown here:

```
package com.packtpub.microservices.ch05.message.clients;

import com.packtpub.microservices.ch05.models.Friendships;
import org.springframework.web.client.RestTemplate;

import java.util.List;

public class SocialGraphClient {
    private String baseUrl;

    public SocialGraphClient(String baseUrl) {
        this.baseUrl = baseUrl;
    }

    public List<String> getFriendships(String username) {
        String requestUrl = baseUrl + "/friendships/" + username;
        RestTemplate template = new RestTemplate();
        UserFriendships friendships =
template.getForObject(requestUrl, UserFriendships.class);
        return friendships.getFriendships();
    }
}
```

5. Let's create our models. We'll need a model to represent `UserFriendships` that a specific user has as well as a model to represent `Messages`. Create a new package called `com.packtpub.microservices.ch05.models` and a new class called `Friendships` as shown here:

```
package com.packtpub.microservices.ch05.models;

import java.util.List;

public class Friendships {
    private String username;
    private List<String> friendships;
```

```
public Friendships() {
    this.friendships = new ArrayList<>();
}

public Friendships(String username) {
    this.username = username;
    this.friendships = new ArrayList<>();
}

public Friendships(String username, List<String> friendships) {
    this.username = username;
    this.friendships = friendships;
}

public String getUsername() {
    return username;
}

public void setUsername(String username) {
    this.username = username;
}

public List<String> getFriendships() {
    return friendships;
}

public void setFriendships(List<String> friendships) {
    this.friendships = friendships;
}
}
```

6. Create a new class, in the same package, called `Message` as shown here:

```
package com.packtpub.microservices.ch05.message.models;

import com.fasterxml.jackson.annotation.JsonProperty;

public class Message {
    private String id;
    private String sender;
    private String recipient;
    private String body;
    @JsonProperty("attachment_uri")
    private String attachmentUri;

    public Message() {}

    public Message(String sender, String recipient, String body,
```

```
String attachmentUri) {
        this.sender = sender;
        this.recipient = recipient;
        this.body = body;
        this.attachmentUri = attachmentUri;
    }

    public Message(String id, String sender, String recipient,
String body, String attachmentUri) {
        this.id = id;
        this.sender = sender;
        this.recipient = recipient;
        this.body = body;
        this.attachmentUri = attachmentUri;
    }

    public String getId() {
        return id;
    }

    public String getSender() {
        return sender;
    }

    public void setSender(String sender) {
        this.sender = sender;
    }

    public String getRecipient() {
        return recipient;
    }

    public void setRecipient(String recipient) {
        this.recipient = recipient;
    }

    public String getBody() {
        return body;
    }

    public void setBody(String body) {
        this.body = body;
    }

    public String getAttachmentUri() {
        return attachmentUri;
    }
```

```
    public void setAttachmentUri(String attachmentUri) {
        this.attachmentUri = attachmentUri;
    }
}
```

7. With our models created, we can now move on to our in-memory message repository. This class simply uses `HashMap` to store messages keyed by `UUID`. These messages are not durable and will not survive a restart of the service, so this is not a recommended technique for a production service. The class has two methods: `saved`, which generates UUID and stores a message in the map, and `get`, which attempts to retrieve a message from the map. If no message is found, an exception is thrown, as shown here:

```
package com.packtpub.microservices.ch05.message;

import
com.packtpub.microservices.ch05.message.exceptions.MessageNotFoundE
xception;
import com.packtpub.microservices.ch05.message.models.Message;

import java.util.HashMap;
import java.util.Map;
import java.util.UUID;

public class MessageRepository {

    private Map<String, Message> messages;

    public MessageRepository() {
        messages = new HashMap<>();
    }

    public Message save(Message message) {
        UUID uuid = UUID.randomUUID();
        Message saved = new Message(uuid.toString(),
message.getSender(), message.getRecipient(),
                message.getBody(), message.getAttachmentUri());
        messages.put(uuid.toString(), saved);
        return saved;
    }

    public Message get(String id) throws MessageNotFoundException {
        if (messages.containsKey(id)) {
            Message message = messages.get(id);
            return message;
        } else {
            throw new MessageNotFoundException("Message " + id + "
```

```
could not be found");
        }
    }
}
```

8. Our service has a single controller for messages. The controller has two endpoints, one that allows a caller to retrieve a message by ID (or a `404` response if the message is not found) and another that attempts to send a message (or a `403` response if the sender and recipient of the message are not friends):

```java
package com.packtpub.microservices.ch05.message;

import
com.packtpub.microservices.ch05.message.clients.SocialGraphClient;
import
com.packtpub.microservices.ch05.message.exceptions.MessageNotFoundE
xception;
import
com.packtpub.microservices.ch05.message.exceptions.MessageSendForbi
ddenException;
import com.packtpub.microservices.ch05.message.models.Message;
import org.springframework.beans.factory.annotation.Autowired;
import org.springframework.http.ResponseEntity;
import org.springframework.web.bind.annotation.*;
import
org.springframework.web.servlet.support.ServletUriComponentsBuilder
;

import java.net.URI;
import java.util.List;

@RestController
public class MessageController {

    @Autowired
    private MessageRepository messagesStore;

    @Autowired
    private SocialGraphClient socialGraphClient;

    @RequestMapping(path = "/messages/{id}", method =
RequestMethod.GET, produces = "application/json")
    public Message get(@PathVariable("id") String id) throws
MessageNotFoundException {
        return messagesStore.get(id);
    }

    @RequestMapping(path = "/messages", method =
```

```
RequestMethod.POST, produces = "application/json")
    public ResponseEntity<Message> send(@RequestBody Message
message) throws MessageSendForbiddenException {

        List<String> friendships =
socialGraphClient.getFriendships(message.getSender());
        if (!friendships.contains(message.getRecipient())) {
            throw new MessageSendForbiddenException("Must be
friends to send message");
        }

        Message saved = messagesStore.save(message);
        URI location = ServletUriComponentsBuilder
                .fromCurrentRequest().path("/{id}")
                .buildAndExpand(saved.getId()).toUri();
        return ResponseEntity.created(location).build();
    }
}
```

9. Create a `Application` class that simply runs our application and creates the necessary beans that get wired into our controller, as shown here:

```
package com.packtpub.microservices.ch05.message;

import
com.packtpub.microservices.ch05.message.clients.SocialGraphClient;
import org.springframework.boot.SpringApplication;
import
org.springframework.boot.autoconfigure.SpringBootApplication;
import org.springframework.context.annotation.Bean;

@SpringBootApplication
public class Application {
    @Bean
    public MessageRepository messageRepository() {
        return new MessageRepository();
    }

    @Bean
    public SocialGraphClient socialGraphClient() {
        return new SocialGraphClient("http://localhost:4567");
    }
}
```

```
public static void main(String[] args) {
    SpringApplication.run(Main.class, args);
}
}
```

This service works, and meets our primary requirement that a message cannot be sent if the sender and recipient are not friends, but it is susceptible to all the problems we described. If the social-graph-service is experiencing problems, the message service will be dependent on timeouts in the `RestTemplate` client, which will impact the number of requests the message service is able to serve. Furthermore, if the social-graph-service is overwhelmed and starts returning `503` (an HTTP status code meant to indicate that a service is temporarily unavailable) the message service has no mechanism to allow the social-graph-service to recover. Let's now introduce the `resilience4j` circuit-breaker library and wrap calls to the social-graph-service:

1. Open `build.gradle` and add the `resilience4j` circuit-breaker library to the list of dependencies, as shown here:

   ```
   ...
   dependencies {
       testCompile group: 'junit', name: 'junit', version: '4.12'
       compile group: 'io.github.resilience4j', name: 'resilience4j-
   circuitbreaker', version: '0.11.0'
       compile group: 'org.springframework.boot', name: 'spring-boot-
   starter-web'
   }
   ...
   ```

2. Modify `SocialGraphClient` to use `CircuitBreaker` when invoking the social-graph-client. In the event that the `SocialGraphClient` returns a failure, we'll return an empty `Friendships` instance, which will cause our service to respond to the user request with a `403` forbidden (default closed). We'll use the default configuration for circuit breakers here, but you should consult the documentation for `resilience4j`, which contains plenty of information about configuring circuit breakers to suit the specific needs of your service. Take a look at this code:

   ```
   package com.packtpub.microservices.ch05.clients;

   import com.packtpub.microservices.ch05.models.Friendships;
   import io.github.resilience4j.circuitbreaker.CircuitBreaker;
   import
   io.github.resilience4j.circuitbreaker.CircuitBreakerRegistry;
   import io.vavr.CheckedFunction0;
   import io.vavr.control.Try;
   ```

```java
import org.springframework.web.client.RestTemplate;

import java.util.List;

public class SocialGraphClient {
    private String baseUrl;

    private CircuitBreaker circuitBreaker;

    public SocialGraphClient(String baseUrl) {
        this.baseUrl = baseUrl;
        this.circuitBreaker =
CircuitBreaker.ofDefaults("socialGraphClient");
    }

    public List<String> getFriendships(String username) {

        CheckedFunction0<Friendships> decoratedSupplier =
CircuitBreaker.decorateCheckedSupplier(circuitBreaker, () -> {
            String requestUrl = baseUrl + "/friendships/" +
username;
            RestTemplate template = new RestTemplate();
            return template.getForObject(requestUrl,
Friendships.class);
        });

        Try<Friendships> result = Try.of(decoratedSupplier);

        return result.getOrElse(new
Friendships(username)).getFriendships();
    }
}
```

Now our service wraps dangerous network calls in a circuit breaker, preventing failures in the social-graph-service from cascading to the message service. In the event of a temporary failure in the social-graph-service, the message service will eventually fail fast and allow the social-graph-service time to recover. You can test this by forcing the mock-social-graph service to return an error code—that's left as a fun exercise for the reader!

Retrying requests with exponential backoff

Failure in distributed systems is inevitable. Instead of trying to prevent failure entirely, we want to design systems that are capable of self-repair. To accomplish this, it is essential to have a good strategy for clients to follow when initiating retries. A service may become temporarily unavailable or experience a problem that requires manual response from an on-call engineer. In either scenario, clients should be able to queue and then retry requests to be given the best chance of success.

Retrying endlessly in the event of an error is not an effective tactic. Imagine a service starts to experience a higher-than-normal failure rate, perhaps even failing 100% of requests. If clients all continuously enqueue retries without ever giving up, you'll end up with a thundering-herd problem—clients continuously retrying requests without limit. As the timeline of the failure progresses, more clients will experience failures, resulting in more retries. You'll end up with a traffic pattern, illustrated by the following diagram, which is a similar graph to the one you'll see during a denial-of-service attack. The end result will be the same—cascading failures due to overwhelmed services and a shedding of legitimate traffic. Your application will become unusable and the failing service will be harder to isolate and repair:

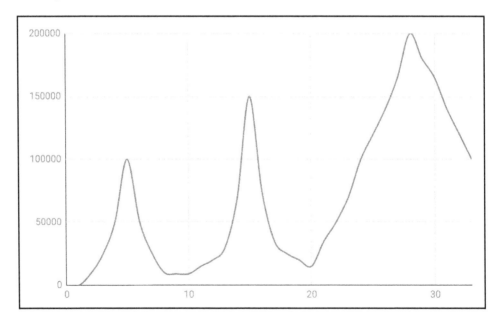

The solution to prevent thundering herds is to add a backoff algorithm that exponentially increases the wait period between retries and gives up after a certain number of failures. This approach is referred to as capped exponential backoff. Adding an exponentially-increasing sleep function between retries accomplishes half of what we're after—clients will slow down their retry attempts, distributing load over time. Unfortunately, client retries will still be clustered, resulting in periods of time where your service is being hammered by many concurrent requests. The second half of our strategy addresses this problem by adding a randomized value or jitter to our sleep function to distribute the retries over time. To summarize, our retry strategy has the following three requirements:

- Retries must be spaced out using an exponential backoff
- Retries must be randomized by adding jitter
- Retries must terminate after a specific amount of time

Most HTTP libraries will have support for a retry strategy that meets these requirements. In this recipe, we'll look at the HTTP `client` library for Java written by Google.

How to do it...

1. To demonstrate using exponential backoff and jitter, we're going to create a sample service in Ruby that has one simple job: to return an HTTP status that indicates a failure. In previous recipes, we've used the `sinatra` Ruby library to do this, so we'll continue with this, a service that simply returns a `503` HTTP status code for every request, as shown here:

```
require 'sinatra'

get '/' do
  halt 503
end
```

2. Create an HTTP client using the Google HTTP `client` Library. First, create a new Gradle Java project with the following `build.gradle` file that imports the necessary libraries and plugins, as shown here:

```
group 'com.packtpub.microservices'
version '1.0-SNAPSHOT'

apply plugin: 'java'
apply plugin: 'application'

mainClassName = 'com.packtpub.microservices.ch05.retryclient.Main'
```

```
sourceCompatibility = 1.8

repositories {
    mavenCentral()
}

dependencies {
    compile group: 'com.google.http-client', name: 'google-http-
client', version: '1.23.0'
    testCompile group: 'junit', name: 'junit', version: '4.12'
}
```

3. Create a new package called
   com.packtpub.microservices.ch05.retryclient. Create a new class called
   Main. In the Main class, we're just going to create an HTTP request and execute
   it. If the request was successful, we'll just print its status code with a nice
   message. If the success fails, we'll still print its status code, but with a message
   indicating that something went wrong. The first version of our HTTP client will
   not attempt any retries. The purpose of this code is to write the simplest client
   possible, not to show off the features of the Google HTTP client library, but I
   encourage you to consult the documentation for the project to learn more about
   it. Let's take a look at the following code:

```
package com.packtpub.microservices.ch05.retryclient;

import com.google.api.client.http.*;
import com.google.api.client.http.javanet.NetHttpTransport;
import com.google.api.client.util.ExponentialBackOff;

import java.io.IOException;

public class Main {

    static final HttpTransport transport = new NetHttpTransport();

    public static void main(String[] args) {
        HttpRequestFactory factory =
transport.createRequestFactory();
        GenericUrl url = new GenericUrl("http://localhost:4567/");

        try {
            HttpRequest request = factory.buildGetRequest(url);
            HttpResponse response = request.execute();
            System.out.println("Got a successful response: " +
response.getStatusCode());
        } catch (HttpResponseException e) {
```

```
                System.out.println("Got an unsuccessful response: " +
e.getStatusCode());
            } catch (IOException e) {
                e.printStackTrace();
            }
        }
    }
```

4. If you run the preceding code either with your IDE or by running `./gradlew`
   `run` from your command line, you'll see that the code tries to make a single
   HTTP request, receives 503 from our Ruby service, and then gives up. Let's now
   instrument it with a configurable backoff that has a randomization factor for
   adding jitter, as shown here:

```
package com.packtpub.microservices.ch05.retryclient;

import com.google.api.client.http.*;
import com.google.api.client.http.javanet.NetHttpTransport;
import com.google.api.client.util.ExponentialBackOff;

import java.io.IOException;

public class Main {

    static final HttpTransport transport = new NetHttpTransport();

    public static void main(String[] args) {
        HttpRequestFactory factory =
transport.createRequestFactory();
        GenericUrl url = new GenericUrl("http://localhost:4567/");

        try {
            HttpRequest request = factory.buildGetRequest(url);
            ExponentialBackOff backoff = new
ExponentialBackOff.Builder()
                    .setInitialIntervalMillis(500)
                    .setMaxElapsedTimeMillis(10000)
                    .setMaxIntervalMillis(6000)
                    .setMultiplier(1.5)
                    .setRandomizationFactor(0.5)
                    .build();

            request.setUnsuccessfulResponseHandler(
              new HttpBackOffUnsuccessfulResponseHandler(backoff));
            HttpResponse response = request.execute();
            System.out.println("Got a successful response: " +
response.getStatusCode());
```

```
        } catch (HttpResponseException e) {
            System.out.println("Got an unsuccessful response: " +
e.getStatusCode());
        } catch (IOException e) {
            e.printStackTrace();
        }
    }
}
```

5. If you run the program now and watch the logs of your Ruby service, you'll see that the code makes multiple attempts to make the request, increasing the amount of time it sleeps between retries, before eventually giving up after about 10 seconds. In a real-world setting, this could give the service enough time to possibly recover while not creating a thundering herd that would eliminate any possibility of repair.

Improving performance with caching

Microservices should be designed in such a way that a single service is usually the only thing that reads or writes to a particular data store. In this model, services have full ownership over the domain models involved in the business capability they provide. Having clean boundaries makes it easier to think about the life cycle of data in a system. Some models in our system will change frequently, but many will be read much more often than they are written. In these cases, we can use a cache to store infrequently changed data, saving us from having to make a request to the database every time the object is requested. Database queries are typically more expensive than cache lookups, so it's ideal to use a cache whenever possible.

In addition to help improve performance, having an effective caching layer can help improve the reliability of a service. It's impossible to guarantee 100% availability for a database, so in the event of a database failure, a service can revert to serving cached data. In most cases, it's preferable for a user to receive some data, even if it's old and potentially out of date, than to receive no data at all. Having a cache layer allows you to configure your service to use it as another source of available data to serve to users of your service.

In this recipe, we'll create a simple example service that serves information about users of your application. It will have two endpoints, the first will accept POST requests and will persist a properly formed user to a database. The second will retrieve a user representation by the ID specified. IDs are stored as UUIDs, which is preferable to autoincrementing IDs for many reasons, which we'll go into in later chapters. We'll start with the basic service, then add caching so we can see specifically what steps are required. In this recipe, we'll use Redis, a popular open source in-memory data-structure store that is particular useful for storing key-value pairs.

How to do it...

1. Create a Gradle Java project called caching-user-service with the following `build.gradle` file. Note that we're adding dependencies for **Java Persistence API (JPA)** and a Java MySQL `client` library:

```
group 'com.packtpub.microservices.ch05'
version '1.0-SNAPSHOT'

buildscript {
    repositories {
        mavenCentral()
    }
    dependencies {
        classpath("org.springframework.boot:spring-boot-gradle-
plugin:2.0.0.RELEASE")
    }
}

apply plugin: 'java'
apply plugin: 'org.springframework.boot'

sourceCompatibility = 1.8

repositories {
    mavenCentral()
}

dependencies {
    compile group: 'org.springframework.boot', name: 'spring-boot-
starter-web', version: '2.0.0.RELEASE'
```

```
    compile group: 'org.springframework.boot', name: 'spring-boot-
starter-data-jpa', version: '2.0.0.RELEASE'
    compile group: 'mysql', name: 'mysql-connector-java', version:
'6.0.6'
    testCompile group: 'junit', name: 'junit', version: '4.12'
}
```

2. Create the `Main` class. As usual, this is the main entry point to our application and is pretty simple:

```
package com.packtpub.microservices.ch05.userservice;

import org.springframework.boot.SpringApplication;
import
org.springframework.boot.autoconfigure.SpringBootApplication;

@SpringBootApplication
public class Main {
    public static void main(String[] args) {
        SpringApplication.run(Main.class, args);
    }
}
```

3. Create a `User` class in the `com.packtpub.microservices.ch05.userservice.models` package. This will serve as our entity representation and contains the fields that will be stored in the database and eventually in our Redis cache:

```
package com.packtpub.microservices.ch05.userservice.models;

import com.fasterxml.jackson.annotation.JsonProperty;
import org.hibernate.annotations.GenericGenerator;

import javax.persistence.Column;
import javax.persistence.Entity;
import javax.persistence.GeneratedValue;
import javax.persistence.Id;

@Entity
public class User {

    @Id
    @GeneratedValue(generator = "uuid")
    @GenericGenerator(name = "uuid", strategy = "uuid2")
    private String id;

    private String username;
```

```java
@JsonProperty("full_name")
private String fullName;

private String email;

public User() {}

public String getId() {
    return id;
}

public void setId(String id) {
    this.id = id;
}

public String getUsername() {
    return username;
}

public void setUsername(String username) {
    this.username = username;
}

public String getFullName() {
    return fullName;
}

public void setFullName(String fullName) {
    this.fullName = fullName;
}

public String getEmail() {
    return email;
}

public void setEmail(String email) {
    this.email = email;
}
}
```

4. To wire up our `User` entity to our MySQL database, create a `UserRepository` interface that extends the `CrudRepository` interface defined by the `springframework` data package, as shown here:

```
package com.packtpub.microservices.ch05.userservice.db;

import com.packtpub.microservices.ch05.userservice.models.User;
import org.springframework.data.repository.CrudRepository;

public interface UserRepository extends CrudRepository<User,
String> {}
```

5. Create the `UserController` class. This is `RestController`, which maps certain endpoints to the functionality discussed previously, namely creating and retrieving user records. Everything here should look familiar. Of note is that the `findById` method returns `Optional<T>`, so we use `map` and `orElseGet` to return either a `200 OK HTTP` response with the user in the response body or a `404` status, as shown in the following code:

```
package com.packtpub.microservices.ch05.userservice.controllers;

import
com.packtpub.microservices.ch05.userservice.db.UserRepository;
import com.packtpub.microservices.ch05.userservice.models.User;
import org.springframework.beans.factory.annotation.Autowired;
import org.springframework.http.HttpStatus;
import org.springframework.http.ResponseEntity;
import org.springframework.web.bind.annotation.*;

import java.util.Optional;

@RestController
public class UserController {

    @Autowired
    private UserRepository userRepository;

    @RequestMapping(path = "/users", method = RequestMethod.POST,
produces = "application/json")
    public User create(@RequestBody User user) {
        User savedUser = userRepository.save(user);
        return savedUser;
    }

    @RequestMapping(path = "/users/{id}", method =
RequestMethod.GET, produces = "application/json")
```

```
    public ResponseEntity<User> getById(@PathVariable("id") String
id) {
        Optional<User> user = userRepository.findById(id);

        return user.map(u -> new ResponseEntity<>(u,
HttpStatus.OK)).orElseGet(
                () -> new ResponseEntity<>(HttpStatus.NOT_FOUND));
    }
}
```

6. Add the following `application.properties` file to the `src/main/resources` directory. It contains the necessary configuration to connect to a local MySQL instance. It's assumed that you have installed MySQL and have it running locally. You should have also created a database called `users`, a user with the username `userservice`, and a password: `password`. Note that we're setting `ddl-auto` to `create`, which is a good practice for development, but should not be used for production:

```
spring.jpa.hibernate.ddl-auto=create
spring.datasource.url=jdbc:mysql://localhost:3306/users?serverTimez
one=UTC&&&useSSL=false
spring.datasource.username=userservice
spring.datasource.password=password
```

7. Let's add some caching! The first thing we'll do is open the `application.properties` file again and add some configuration for a `redis` instance running locally on port `6379` (the default), as shown here:

```
spring.jpa.hibernate.ddl-auto=create
spring.datasource.url=jdbc:mysql://localhost:3306/users?serverTimez
one=UTC&&&useSSL=false
spring.datasource.username=userservice
spring.datasource.password=password
spring.cache.type=redis
spring.redis.host=localhost
spring.redis.port=6379
```

8. With our application configured to use MySQL as a primary datasource and Redis as a cache, we can now override methods in the `CrudRepository<T, ID>` interface and add annotations instructing it to cache. We want to write to our cache every time we call the `save` method with a `User` object, and read from the cache every time we call `findById` with a valid user ID string:

```
package com.packtpub.microservices.ch05.userservice.db;

import com.packtpub.microservices.ch05.userservice.models.User;
import org.springframework.cache.annotation.CachePut;
import org.springframework.cache.annotation.Cacheable;
import org.springframework.data.repository.CrudRepository;
import org.springframework.stereotype.Repository;

import java.util.Optional;

@Repository
public interface UserRepository extends CrudRepository<User,
String> {
    @Override
    @Cacheable(value = "users", key = "#id")
    Optional<User> findById(String id);

    @Override
    @CachePut(value = "users", key = "#user.id")
    User save(User user);
}
```

9. That's it! You can test this by running the service, creating a user, verifying that the user is in both the MySQL database and Redis cache, and then deleting the user from the database. Requests to the `users/ID` endpoint will still return the user record. Before finishing this service, you'll want to make sure that the cache is invalidated if a user is ever deleted. Any other endpoints that mutate users should invalidate and/or rewrite the cache. This is left as an exercise for the reader!

Fronting your services with a CDN

The **Content Delivery Network** (**CDN**) improves performance and availability by delivering content through a globally distributed network of proxy servers. When a user (usually through their mobile device) makes a request to your API through a CDN, they will create a network connection with one of many **points of presence** (**PoPs**), based on their geographic location. Instead of having to make roundtrips to the origin data center for every single request, content can be cached at the edge of a CDN, greatly reducing the response time for the user and reducing unnecessary, costly traffic to the origin.

CDNs are a requirement if you plan to have a global user base. If every request to your application's API has to perform a full roundtrip to a single origin, you'll create a subpar experience for users in parts of the world physically distant from the data center that you host your applications in. Even if you host your applications in multiple data centers, you'll never be able to create as high-performing an experience for as many users as you can using a CDN.

In addition to performance, CDNs can improve the availability of your application. As we discussed in the previous recipe, many entities in your system are read much more frequently than they are written. In these cases, you can configure your CDN to cache payloads from a service for a specific amount of time (commonly specified by a TTL or time-to-live). Caching responses from your service reduces the amount of traffic to your origin, making it harder to run out of capacity (compute, storage, or network). Additionally, if your service starts to experience high latency, or total or partial failure, the CDN can be configured to serve cached responses instead of continuing to send traffic to a failing service. This allows you to at least be able to serve content to users in the event of service downtime.

Some CDN providers have APIs that allow you to automatically invalidate a resource. In these cases, you can instrument your microservice to invalidate a resource just as you would using a Redis- or Memcached-based cache, as discussed in the previous recipe.

There are many different CDN providers out there. Some of the large ones include **Akamai** and **Edgecast**. Amazon Web Services provides a CDN offering, called CloudFront, that can be configured to serve requests to origin servers in AWS or static resources hosted in S3 buckets. One of the more developer-friendly offerings in the CDN market is from a company called **Fastly**. Fastly is built using **Varnish**, an open source web-application accelerator.

As a provider, Fastly allows you to upload your own **Varnish Configuration Language** (**VCL**) files, effectively allowing you to create caching rules based on any aspect of the request (incoming headers, path segments, query string parameters, and so on). Additionally, Fastly provide a **Fast Purge API** that allows you to invalidate resources based on a URI.

In this recipe, we'll go through the basic steps required to create an account with a CDN provider and start serving traffic through a CDN. We'll do this with a hypothetical service made accessible to the public internet with the hostname `api.pichat.me`. The service authenticates requests by inspecting the value of the Authorization header of the incoming request for a valid OAuth2 bearer token.

How to do it...

1. Create an account with Fastly, the CDN provider we'll be using in this example. As of this writing, the signup URL is `https://www.fastly.com/signup`.
2. Fastly will ask you to create a service. Enter a name for your service, along with the domain (`api.pichat.me`) and the hostname of the origin server the application is running on.
3. Using your DNS provider for the domain, create a CNAME for `api.pichat.me`, pointing your domain to Fastly's servers. Read the updated documentation to find out what hostnames to use.
4. Once that is set up and your service is created, requests to your hostname will now go through the Fastly CDN. Read the Fastly documentation (`https://docs.fastly.com/guides/basic-setup/`) to discover how to customize VCLs and other settings for your service.

Gracefully degrading the user experience

We understand by now that a certain amount of failure is inevitable. In a sufficiently complex system, some amount of failure will occur some of the time. By using the techniques in this chapter, we can try and reduce the likelihood that one of these failures will impact customers. Regardless of how much we try to prevent it from happening, some kind of failure will probably impact the customer experience at some point in your applications lifespan. Users, however, can be surprisingly compassionate in the face of system outages, provided the user experience degrades gracefully.

Consider this scenario: you are using an application that allows you to browse a catalog of products and look for local stores that carry that product, along with important information such as its address, phone number, and store hours. Let's say the service that provides information about local stores becomes unavailable. This clearly impacts the user experience in a less-than-ideal way, but the application can handle the failure in more than one way. The worst way, which would probably result in the worst user experience, would be to allow the failure to cascade and take down the product catalog. A slightly better way would be to allow the user to continue searching for products, but when they go to find a local store that carries the product, they're informed via some kind of information box that the local store information is currently unavailable. This is frustrating, but at least they can still look at product information, such as price, models, and colors. It would be better still to recognize that the service was not operating and have some kind of informational banner informing the user that local store information is temporarily unavailable. With this information, we can inform the user of the situation, allowing them to decide whether they'd still like to go ahead and search for products. The experience is suboptimal, but we would avoid unnecessarily frustrating the user.

Verifying fault tolerance with Gameday exercises

This chapter contains recipes that should help you create more reliable, resilient microservice architectures. Each recipe documents a pattern or technique for anticipating and dealing with some kind of failure scenario. Our aim when building resilient systems is to tolerate failure with as little impact to our users as possible. Anticipating and designing for failure is essential when building distributed systems, but without verifying that our systems handle failure in the ways we expect, we aren't doing much more than hoping, and hope is definitely not a strategy!

When building systems, unit and functional tests are necessary parts of our confidence-building toolkit. However, these tools alone are not enough. Unit and functional tests work by isolating dependencies, good unit tests, for instance, don't rely on network conditions, and functional tests don't involve testing under production-level traffic conditions, instead focusing on various software components working together properly under ideal conditions. To gain more confidence in the fault tolerance of a system, it's necessary to observe it responding to failure in production.

Gameday exercises are another useful tool for building confidence in the resiliency of a system. These exercises involve forcing certain failure scenarios in production to verify that our assumptions about fault tolerance match reality. John Allspaw describes this practice in detail in his paper, *Fault Injection in Production*. If we accept that failure is impossible to avoid completely, it becomes sensible to force failure and observe how our system responds to it as a planned exercise. It's better to have a system fail for the first time while an entire team is watching and ready to take action, than at 3 a.m. when a system alert wakes up an on-call engineer.

Planning a Gameday exercise provides a large amount of value. Engineers should get together and brainstorm the various failure scenarios their service is likely to experience. Work should then be scheduled to try to reduce or eliminate the impact of those scenarios (that is, in the event of database failure, revert to a cache). Each Gameday exercise should have a planning document that describes the system being tested, the various failure scenarios, including steps that will be taken to simulate the failures, expectations surrounding how the system should respond to the failures, and the expected impact on users (if any). As the Gameday exercise proceeds, the team should work through each of the scenarios, documenting observations—it's important to ensure that metrics we expect to see emitted are being emitted, alerts that we expect to fire do indeed fire, and the failure is handled in the way we expect. As observations are made, document any differences between expectations and reality. These observations should become planned work to bridge the gap between our ideal world and the real world.

Instead of walking through code, this recipe will demonstrate a process and template that can be used to run Gameday exercises. The following is not the only way to conduct Gameday exercises, but one that should serve as a good starting point for your organization.

Prerequisites

As always, there are some prerequisites you should ensure you meet before attempting to run a Gameday exercise. Specifically, your teams should be used to instrumenting code with the necessary metrics and alerts to provide a good degree of observability into your production environment. Your teams should have experience working within a well-understood and practiced incident-response process that includes having regular retrospectives to continuously improve in light of production incidents.

Finally, your organization should be accustomed to talking openly about failure and unexpected production incidents, and be committed to processes that encourage continuous improvement. These prerequisites should suggest that your teams have the necessary organizational support and psychological safety to conduct these kinds of resiliency exercises.

How to do it...

1. The first step in a Gameday exercise is selecting a system that will be tested. When you're just getting started with Gamedays, it's wise to select a system that is well understood, has failed before, and has a limited blast radius in terms of the impact on users.

2. Once the service is selected, gather the team responsible for its development and operation, and start brainstorming different failure scenarios. If there is a data store, consider what could happen if it were suddenly unavailable due to a hardware failure. Perhaps the database could be shut down manually. What happens if the database is terminated in an unsafe way? The service runs in some kind of clustered configuration, so what happens if one node is removed from the load balancer? What happens when all nodes fail and are removed from the load-balancing pool? Another area to test is unexpected latency. In a distributed system, sufficiently high latency is impossible to distinguish from lack of service availability, so there are a number of interesting bugs that can lurk here. Getting the team together to discuss all of these scenarios (as well as others) can be a great way to learn more about a system. Document all of the scenarios that you plan to test.

3. Schedule a time and a room for the Gameday experiment (if you're a remote team, arrange for everyone to be on a video call together). Invite the team responsible for the service being tested, a representative from your customer support team, and any other stakeholders who are interested in seeing the experiment.

4. Using a template, such as the one included here, plan out in detail how the experiment is going to be conducted. On the day at the scheduled time, start with an overview of the system being tested. This is a good opportunity to ensure that everyone has a consistent view of how the system works. Then go through each scenario, assigning the actual action to someone on the team.

5. Document observations during the experiment, detailing how the system reacted to the failure injection.

6. In the event that observations made during the experiment are different than expectations, schedule follow-up tasks, in the form of tickets, for the team to correct the discrepancy.

A template for Gameday exercises

The following template can be used for planning and executing a Gameday exercise.

System: Message Service

System Overview:

A detailed description (possibly including diagrams) of the system under test. It's a good idea to document how requests are routed to the system, some of the major systems that interact with it, data stores it uses and their general configuration, and any downstream services it depends on.

Dashboards:

Links to important dashboards to watch while the Gameday exercise is underway.

Test Scenarios:

Scenario: Database becomes unavailable due to nodes being terminated.

Method:

Shut down database EC2 nodes manually using AWS CLI tools (include actual command).

Expectations:

List how you expect the service to react. Include details about expected changes in metrics, alerts that should be fired, system behavior, and user impact.

Observations:

Document observations during the actual test.

Follow-up Action Items:

Create tickets for any follow-up work that should be done as a result of the experiment.

Introducing automated chaos

Running manual Gameday exercises is a great way to introduce the practice of failure injection. Forcing failures in production helps build confidence in the resilience of systems and identifies opportunities for improvement. Gameday helps teams gain a better overall understanding of how their systems behave when confronted with a number of failure scenarios. As a team conducts more exercises, it will start to accumulate tools for performing common tasks, such as introducing latency in the network or spiking CPU usage. Tooling helps automate mundane tasks, improving the efficiency of Gameday exercises. There are a variety of open source and commercial tools designed to automate chaos engineering that teams can take advantage of right away.

Gameday exercises are planned and scheduled. Some organizations go one step further and introduce continuous failure injection as a way of ensuring that systems are handling common failure scenarios smoothly. In early 2011, Netflix announced the creation of the Simian Army—a suite of tools designed to inject common failures into a production environment. Arguably the most famous member of the Simian Army, Chaos Monkey, randomly shuts down nodes in a production environment. The Simian Army tools have been open sourced and are available to use in your own organization. They can be scheduled to run as part of a Gameday exercise, or set up to run on specific schedules (that is, Monday to Friday, 9 a.m. to 5 p.m., when on-call engineers are usually in the office).

Pioneers in this space, PagerDuty, have conducted "failure Fridays" since 2013. Every Friday, engineers get together to attack a specific service. Over time, engineers started building commands into their Chat Bot to perform common functions such as isolating a node from other network traffic, even adding a "roulette" command that would randomly select hosts for rebooting.

Hosted commercial services have been developed to help automate chaos engineering. Gremlin is a hosted product designed to help teams run Gameday exercises by providing access to a library of "attacks" executed through agents installed on nodes in your environment. Gremlin provides an API and a web interface that allows users to configure attacks designed to spike resource usage (CPU, memory, disk), simulate random failures by killing processes or rebooting hosts, and simulate common network conditions, such as latency and **Network Time Protocol** (NTP) drift. Having a product like Gremlin lowers the amount of upfront effort needed to start doing failure injection.

Another open source tool is the Chaos toolkit, a CLI tool designed to make it easier to design and run experiments. In this recipe, we'll install the Chaos toolkit and use it to execute a simple experiment against a hypothetical user service. The user service will be the same one we wrote in the *Improving performance with caching* recipe earlier in this chapter.

How to do it...

1. The Chaos toolkit is written in Python and can be installed using `pip`. We'll need a working Python3 environment. This recipe will assume you are installing it on macOS X using Homebrew. First, install `pyen`—a utility that supports managing multiple Python development environments, as shown here:

   ```
   $ brew install pyenv
   ```

2. Install Python3 by executing the following command line:

   ```
   $ pyenv install 3.4.2
   $ pyenv global 3.4.2
   ```

3. With a newly-installed Python3 environment, go ahead and install the Chaos toolkit by executing the following command line:

   ```
   $ pip install -U chaostoolkit
   ```

4. The Chaos toolkit uses the JSON files to describe experiments. Each experiment should have a title, description, and optionally some tags used to categorize experiments. The `steady-state-hypothesis` section describes how the service is expected to behave under normal conditions. In our situation, we assume that the service will return either `200` in the event that a user is found, or `404` in the event that a user has not been found:

   ```
   {
     "title": "Kill MySQL process",
     "description": "The user service uses a MySQL database to store
   user information. This experiment will test how the service behaves
   when the database is unavailable.",
     "tags": [
       "database", "mysql"
     ],
     "steady-state-hypothesis": {
       "title": "Service responds when MySQL is running",
       "probes": [
         {
           "type": "probe",
   ```

```
        "name": "service-is-running",
        "tolerance": [200, 404],
        "provider": {
          "type": "http",
          "url": "http://localhost:8080/users/12345"
        }
      }
    ]
  },
  "method": [
    {
      "name": "kill-mysql-process",
      "type": "action",
      "provider": {
        "type": "process",
        "path": "/usr/local/bin/mysql.server",
        "arguments": ["stop"],
        "timeout": 10
      }
    }
  ]
}
```

5. Run this experiment:

   ```
   $ chaos run
   ```

6. If successful, the output should indicate that the service responds well when
   MySQL is unavailable. However, in its current state, the experiment will leave
   MySQL stopped, which isn't ideal. Now you have something to fix, which is left
   as an exercise to the reader, and you can rerun your experiment.
   Congratulations! You just ran your first automated chaos experiment.

6
Security

In this chapter, we will cover the following recipes:

- Authenticating your microservices
- Securing containers
- Secure configuration
- Secure logging
- Infrastructure as Code

Introduction

As with many of the topics covered in this book, security in a microservice architecture is about trade-offs. In a microservice architecture, individual code bases have limited responsibilities. If an attacker is able to compromise a single running service, they will only be able to perform actions that are governed by that particular microservice. The distributed nature of a microservice architecture, however, means that there are more targets for an attacker to potentially exploit in services running in separate clusters. The network traffic between those clusters, including traffic between edge services and internal services, presents many opportunities for an attacker to discover vulnerabilities.

Because of the distributed nature of microservice architectures, network topology must be considered when configuring how services are able to communicate with one another. This concern exists in monolithic code bases as well, where a running instance of a single code base needs to communicate over the network with database servers, caches, load balancers, and so on. It could be argued that microservice architectures make these challenges more obvious and therefore force engineers to consider them earlier.

Security is a big topic. This chapter will discuss a number of good practices to consider when building, deploying, and operating microservices, but it's important to note that this is not an exhaustive list of considerations. Good API practices and defense in depth should be considered when developing any system and microservices are no exception. I heartily recommend **OWASP** (`https://www.owasp.org/index.php/Main_Page`) as a resource for learning more about web application security.

Authenticating your microservices

In `Chapter 1`, *Breaking the Monolith*, we introduced a Ruby on Rails code base that powers our fictional image-sharing application, `pichat`. The Rails code base authenticates each request by inspecting the Authorization header. If the header is present, the application attempts to decode it using a shared secret read from an environment variable (see the *Secure configuration* recipe). If the token provided in the Authorization header is valid, the decoded value contains contextual information about the user, including the user ID. That information is then used to retrieve the user from the database so that the application has context on the user making the request. If the Authorization header is missing or cannot be decoded successfully, the application raises an exception and returns an HTTP 401 to the caller, including an error message. In order to obtain a token to include in the Authorization header, a client application can send a `POST` request to the `/auth/login` endpoint with valid user credentials. The following CURL commands demonstrate this flow:

```
$ curl -D - -X POST http://localhost:9292/auth/login -
d'email=p@eval.ca&password=foobar123'

HTTP/1.1 200 OK
Content-Type: application/json; charset=utf-8
ETag: W/"3675d2006d59e01f8665f20ffef65fe7"
Cache-Control: max-age=0, private, must-revalidate
X-Request-Id: 6660a102-059f-4afe-b17c-99375db305dd
X-Runtime: 0.150903
Transfer-Encoding: chunked

{"auth_token":"eyJhbGciOiJIUzI1NiJ9.eyJ1c2VyX21kIjoxLCJleHAiOjE1MzE2ODUxNjR
9.vAToW_mWlOnr-GPzP79EvN62Q2MpsnLIYanz3MTbZ5Q"}
```

Now that we have a token, we can include it in the headers of subsequent requests:

```
$ curl -X POST -D - -H 'Authorization:
eyJhbGciOiJIUzI1NiJ9.eyJ1c2VyX21kIjoxLCJleHAiOjE1MzE2ODUxNjR9.vAToW_mWlOnr-
GPzP79EvN62Q2MpsnLIYanz3MTbZ5Q' http://localhost:9292/messages -
d'body=Hello&user_id=1'
```

```
HTTP/1.1 201 Created
Content-Type: application/json; charset=utf-8
ETag: W/"211cdab551e63ca48de48217357f1cf7"
Cache-Control: max-age=0, private, must-revalidate
X-Request-Id: 1525333c-dada-40ff-8c25-a0e7d151433c
X-Runtime: 0.019609
Transfer-Encoding: chunked

{"id":1,"body":"Hello","user_id":1,"created_at":"2018-07-14T20:08:19.369Z",
"updated_at":"2018-07-14T20:08:19.369Z","from_user_id":1}
```

Because `pichat-api` is a monolithic code base, it is playing many different roles to support this flow. It is acting as an Authorization service, an Authentication gateway, a user store, and an Authorization client. This kind of coupling of responsibilities is exactly what we want to avoid in a microservice architecture.

Luckily, it's easy to divide these responsibilities into separate code bases while keeping the flow the same. Encoding information in **JSON Web Tokens (JWT)** using a shared secret allows individual microservices to securely authenticate requests without having to make requests to a centralized authentication service for each request. Obtaining an authentication token can be the responsibility of a centralized service, but this fact can be made transparent to the client using an API Gateway or a backend for a frontend. The following diagram demonstrates how some of the responsibilities will be divided:

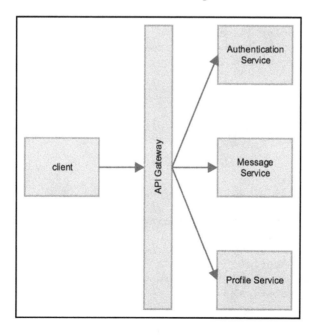

We will create an **Authentication Service** that handles user registration and exchanges credentials for a JWT. We will then create a simple **API Gateway** using the Zuul open source project that we covered in Chapter 2, *Edge Services*.

How to do it...

Let's have a look at the following steps:

1. Let's create the authentication service. Create a new Java project with the following build.gradle file:

```
group 'com.packtpub.microservices'
version '1.0-SNAPSHOT'

buildscript {
    repositories {
        mavenCentral()
    }
    dependencies {
        classpath group: 'org.springframework.boot', name: 'spring-
boot-gradle-plugin', version: '1.5.9.RELEASE'
    }
}

apply plugin: 'java'
apply plugin: 'org.springframework.boot'
apply plugin: 'io.spring.dependency-management'

sourceCompatibility = 1.8

repositories {
    mavenCentral()
}

dependencies {
    compile group: 'org.springframework.boot', name: 'spring-boot-
starter-web'
    compile group: 'org.springframework.security', name: 'spring-
security-core'
    compile group: 'org.springframework.security', name: 'spring-
security-config'
    compile group: 'org.springframework.boot', name: 'spring-boot-
starter-data-jpa'
```

```
    compile group: 'io.jsonwebtoken', name: 'jjwt', version:
'0.9.1'
    compile group: 'mysql', name: 'mysql-connector-java'
    testCompile group: 'junit', name: 'junit', version: '4.12'
}
```

We'll be storing user credentials in a MySQL database, so we declare `mysql-connector-java` as a dependency. We'll also use an open source JWT library called `jjwt`.

Storing user credentials is an important topic. User passwords should never be stored in plain text and many hashing algorithms, such as MD5 and SHA1, have been shown to be vulnerable to various brute force attacks. In this example, we'll be using `bcrypt`. In a real-world usage, we'd consider multiple hashing steps, such as hashing with SHA512 first and then running through `bcrypt`. We'd also consider adding a per-user salt. The **Open Web Application Security Project** has a lot of great recommendations for storing passwords: `https://www.owasp.org/index.php/Password_Storage_Cheat_Sheet`.

2. Create a new class called `Application`. It will contain our main method as well as `PasswordEncoder`:

```
package com.packtpub.microservices.ch06.auth;

import org.springframework.boot.SpringApplication;
import
org.springframework.boot.autoconfigure.SpringBootApplication;
import org.springframework.context.annotation.Bean;
import
org.springframework.security.crypto.bcrypt.BCryptPasswordEncoder;
import
org.springframework.security.crypto.password.PasswordEncoder;

@SpringBootApplication
public class Application {

    @Bean
    public PasswordEncoder passwordEncoder() {
        return new BCryptPasswordEncoder();
    }

    public static void main(String[] args) {
        SpringApplication.run(Application.class, args);
    }
}
```

3. We'll model the user credentials as a simple POJO with email and password fields. Create a new package called com.packtpub.microservices.ch06.auth.models and a new class called UserCredential:

```
package com.packtpub.microservices.ch06.auth.models;

import org.hibernate.annotations.GenericGenerator;

import javax.persistence.*;

@Entity
public class UserCredential {
    @Id
    @GeneratedValue(generator = "uuid")
    @GenericGenerator(name = "uuid", strategy = "uuid2")
    private String id;

    @Column(unique=true)
    private String email;

    private String password;

    public UserCredential(String email) {
        this.email = email;
    }

    public String getId() {
        return id;
    }

    public void setId(String id) {
        this.id = id;
    }

    public String getEmail() {
        return email;
    }

    public void setEmail(String email) {
        this.email = email;
    }

    public String getPassword() {
        return password;
    }
```

```
public void setPassword(String password) {
    this.password = password;
}
}
```

4. Create a model to represent the response to successful login and registration requests. Successful responses will contain a JSON document containing a JWT. Create a new class called `AuthenticationToken`:

```
package com.packtpub.microservices.ch06.auth.models;

import com.fasterxml.jackson.annotation.JsonProperty;

public class AuthenticationToken {

    @JsonProperty("auth_token")
    private String authToken;

    public AuthenticationToken() {}

    public AuthenticationToken(String authToken) {
        this.authToken = authToken;
    }

    public String getAuthToken() {
        return this.authToken;
    }

    public void setAuthToken(String authToken) {
        this.authToken = authToken;
    }
}
```

5. The `UserCredential` class will be accessed using the Java Persistence API. To do this, we have to first create `CrudRepository`. Create a new package called `com.packtpub.microservices.ch06.auth.data` and a new class called `UserCredentialRepository`. In addition to inheriting from `CrudRepository`, we'll define a single method used to retrieve a `UserCredential` instance by email:

```
package com.packtpub.microservices.ch06.auth.data;

import com.packtpub.microservices.ch06.auth.models.UserCredential;
import org.springframework.data.repository.CrudRepository;

public interface UserCredentialRepository extends
CrudRepository<UserCredential, String> {
```

```
       UserCredential findByEmail(String email);
}
```

6. When a user attempts to register or log in with invalid credentials, we want to return an HTTP 401 status code as well as a message indicating that they provided invalid credentials. In order to do this, we'll create a single exception that will be thrown in our controller methods:

```
package com.packtpub.microservices.ch06.auth.exceptions;

import org.springframework.http.HttpStatus;
import org.springframework.web.bind.annotation.ResponseStatus;

@ResponseStatus(HttpStatus.UNAUTHORIZED)
public class InvalidCredentialsException extends Exception {
    public InvalidCredentialsException(String message) {
super(message);  }
}
```

7. Create the controller. The login and registration endpoints will be served from a single controller. The registration method will simply validate input and create a new UserCredential instance, persisting it using the CrudRepository package we created earlier. It will then encode a JWT with the user ID of the newly registered user as the subject. The login method will verify the provided credentials and provide a JWT with the user ID as its subject. The controller will need access to UserCredentialRepository and PasswordEncoder defined in the main class. Create a new package called com.packtpub.microservices.ch06.auth.controllers and a new class called UserCredentialController:

```
package com.packtpub.microservices.ch06.auth.controllers;

import
com.packtpub.microservices.ch06.auth.data.UserCredentialRepository;
import
com.packtpub.microservices.ch06.auth.exceptions.InvalidCredentialsE
xception;
import
com.packtpub.microservices.ch06.auth.models.AuthenticationToken;
import com.packtpub.microservices.ch06.auth.models.UserCredential;
import io.jsonwebtoken.JwtBuilder;
import io.jsonwebtoken.Jwts;
import io.jsonwebtoken.SignatureAlgorithm;
import org.springframework.beans.factory.annotation.Autowired;
import org.springframework.beans.factory.annotation.Value;
import
```

```
org.springframework.security.crypto.password.PasswordEncoder;
import org.springframework.web.bind.annotation.*;

import javax.crypto.spec.SecretKeySpec;
import javax.xml.bind.DatatypeConverter;
import java.security.Key;

@RestController
public class UserCredentialController {

    @Autowired
    private UserCredentialRepository userCredentialRepository;

    @Autowired
    private PasswordEncoder passwordEncoder;

    @Value("${secretKey}")
    private String keyString;

    private String encodeJwt(String userId) {
        System.out.println("SIGNING KEY: " + keyString);
        Key key = new SecretKeySpec(
                DatatypeConverter.parseBase64Binary(keyString),
                SignatureAlgorithm.HS256.getJcaName());

        JwtBuilder builder = Jwts.builder().setId(userId)
                .setSubject(userId)
                .setIssuer("authentication-service")
                .signWith(SignatureAlgorithm.HS256, key);

        return builder.compact();
    }

    @RequestMapping(path = "/register", method =
RequestMethod.POST, produces = "application/json")
    public AuthenticationToken register(@RequestParam String email,
@RequestParam String password, @RequestParam String
passwordConfirmation) throws InvalidCredentialsException {
        if (!password.equals(passwordConfirmation)) {
            throw new InvalidCredentialsException("Password and
confirmation do not match");
        }

        UserCredential cred = new UserCredential(email);
        cred.setPassword(passwordEncoder.encode(password));
        userCredentialRepository.save(cred);

        String jws = encodeJwt(cred.getId());
```

```
            return new AuthenticationToken(jws);
    }

    @RequestMapping(path = "/login", method = RequestMethod.POST,
produces = "application/json")
    public AuthenticationToken login(@RequestParam String email,
@RequestParam String password) throws InvalidCredentialsException {
        UserCredential user =
userCredentialRepository.findByEmail(email);

        if (user == null || !passwordEncoder.matches(password,
user.getPassword())) {
            throw new InvalidCredentialsException("Username or
password invalid");
        }

        String jws = encodeJwt(user.getId());
        return new AuthenticationToken(jws);
    }
}
```

8. Because we are connecting to a local database, and because we use a shared secret when signing JWTs, we need to create a small properties file. Create a file called `application.yml` in the `src/main/resources` directory:

```
server:
  port: 8081

spring:
  jpa.hibernate.ddl-auto: create
  datasource.url: jdbc:mysql://localhost:3306/user_credentials
  datasource.username: root
  datasource.password:

secretKey: supers3cr3t
```

Now that we have a functioning authentication service, the next step is to create a simple API Gateway using the open source gateway service, Zuul. In addition to routing requests to downstream services, the API Gateway will also use an authentication filter to verify that valid JWTs are passed in headers for requests that require authentication.

9. Create a new Java project with the following `build.gradle` file:

```
group 'com.packtpub.microservices'
version '1.0-SNAPSHOT'

buildscript {
    repositories {
        mavenCentral()
    }
    dependencies {
        classpath group: 'org.springframework.boot', name: 'spring-
boot-gradle-plugin', version: '1.5.9.RELEASE'
    }
}

apply plugin: 'java'
apply plugin: 'org.springframework.boot'
apply plugin: 'io.spring.dependency-management'

sourceCompatibility = 1.8
targetCompatibility = 1.8

repositories {
    mavenCentral()
}

dependencyManagement {
    imports {
        mavenBom 'org.springframework.cloud:spring-cloud-
netflix:1.4.4.RELEASE'
    }
}

dependencies {
    compile group: 'org.springframework.boot', name: 'spring-boot-
starter-web'
    compile group: 'org.springframework.cloud', name: 'spring-
cloud-starter-zuul'
    compile group: 'org.springframework.security', name: 'spring-
security-core'
    compile group: 'org.springframework.security', name: 'spring-
security-config'
    compile group: 'org.springframework.security', name: 'spring-
security-web'
    compile group: 'io.jsonwebtoken', name: 'jjwt', version:
'0.9.1'
    testCompile group: 'junit', name: 'junit', version: '4.12'
}
```

Note that we're using the same JWT library as the Authentication service.

10. Create a new package called `com.packtpub.microservices.ch06.gateway` and a new class called `Application`:

```
package com.packtpub.microservices.ch06.gateway;

import org.springframework.boot.SpringApplication;
import
org.springframework.boot.autoconfigure.SpringBootApplication;
import org.springframework.cloud.netflix.zuul.EnableZuulProxy;

@EnableZuulProxy
@SpringBootApplication
public class Application {
    public static void main(String[] args) {
        SpringApplication.run(Application.class, args);
    }
}
```

11. We'll create an authentication filter by creating a subclass of `OncePerRequestFilter`, which aims to provide a single execution per request dispatch. The filter will parse the JWT out of the Authorization header and try to decode it using a shared secret. If the JWT can be verified and decoded, we can be sure that it was encoded by an issuer that had access to the shared secret. We'll treat this as our trust boundary; anyone with access to the shared secret can be trusted, and therefore we can trust that the subject of the JWT is the ID of the authenticated user. Create a new class called `AuthenticationFilter`:

```
package com.packtpub.microservices.ch06.gateway;

import io.jsonwebtoken.Claims;
import io.jsonwebtoken.Jwts;
import
org.springframework.security.authentication.UsernamePasswordAuthent
icationToken;
import org.springframework.security.core.Authentication;
import
org.springframework.security.core.authority.SimpleGrantedAuthority;
import
org.springframework.security.core.context.SecurityContextHolder;
import org.springframework.web.filter.OncePerRequestFilter;
import javax.servlet.FilterChain;
import javax.servlet.ServletException;
import javax.servlet.http.HttpServletRequest;
import javax.servlet.http.HttpServletResponse;
import javax.xml.bind.DatatypeConverter;
```

```java
import java.io.IOException;
import java.util.ArrayList;
import java.util.Optional;

public class AuthenticationFilter extends OncePerRequestFilter {

    private String signingSecret;

    AuthenticationFilter(String signingSecret) {
        this.signingSecret = signingSecret;
    }

    @Override
    protected void doFilterInternal(HttpServletRequest request,
HttpServletResponse response, FilterChain filterChain) throws
ServletException, IOException {
        Optional<String> token =
Optional.ofNullable(request.getHeader("Authorization"));
        Optional<Authentication> auth = token.filter(t ->
t.startsWith("Bearer")).flatMap(this::authentication);
        auth.ifPresent(a ->
SecurityContextHolder.getContext().setAuthentication(a));
        filterChain.doFilter(request, response);
    }

    private Optional<Authentication> authentication(String t) {
        System.out.println(signingSecret);
        String actualToken = t.substring("Bearer ".length());
        try {
            Claims claims = Jwts.parser()
.setSigningKey(DatatypeConverter.parseBase64Binary(signingSecret))
                    .parseClaimsJws(actualToken).getBody();
            Optional<String> userId =
Optional.ofNullable(claims.getSubject()).map(Object::toString);
            return userId.map(u -> new
UsernamePasswordAuthenticationToken(u, null, new
ArrayList<SimpleGrantedAuthority>()));
        } catch (Exception e) {
            return Optional.empty();
        }

    }
}
```

12. Wire this together with a security configuration for the API Gateway project. Create a new class called `SecurityConfig`:

```
package com.packtpub.microservices.ch06.gateway;

import org.springframework.beans.factory.annotation.Value;
import
org.springframework.security.config.annotation.web.builders.HttpSec
urity;
import
org.springframework.security.config.annotation.web.configuration.En
ableWebSecurity;
import
org.springframework.security.config.annotation.web.configuration.We
bSecurityConfigurerAdapter;
import
org.springframework.security.config.http.SessionCreationPolicy;
import
org.springframework.security.web.authentication.UsernamePasswordAut
henticationFilter;

import javax.servlet.http.HttpServletResponse;

@EnableWebSecurity
public class SecurityConfig extends WebSecurityConfigurerAdapter {

    @Value("${jwt.secret}")
    private String signingSecret;

    @Override
    protected void configure(HttpSecurity security) throws
Exception {
        security
            .csrf().disable()
            .logout().disable()
            .formLogin().disable()
.sessionManagement().sessionCreationPolicy(SessionCreationPolicy.ST
ATELESS)
            .and()
                .anonymous()
            .and()
                .exceptionHandling().authenticationEntryPoint(
                    (req, rsp, e) ->
rsp.sendError(HttpServletResponse.SC_UNAUTHORIZED))
            .and()
                .addFilterAfter(new
AuthenticationFilter(signingSecret),
                        UsernamePasswordAuthenticationFilter.class)
```

```
                    .authorizeRequests()
                    .antMatchers("/auth/**").permitAll()
                    .antMatchers("/messages/**").authenticated()
                    .antMatchers("/users/**").authenticated();
          }
      }
```

As we can see, we're permitting any requests to the authentication service (requests prefixed with /auth/...). We require that requests to the users or messages service be authenticated.

13. We need a configuration file to store the shared secret as well as the routing information for the Zuul server. Create a file called application.yml in the src/main/resources directory:

```
server:
  port: 8080

jwt:
  secret: supers3cr3t

zuul:
  routes:
    authentication-service:
      path: /auth/**
      url: http://127.0.0.1:8081
    message-service:
      path: /messages/**
      url: http://127.0.0.1:8082
    user-service:
      path: /users/**
      url: http://127.0.0.1:8083
```

14. Now that we have a working authentication service and an API Gateway capable of verifying JWTs, we can test our authentication scheme by running the API Gateway, authentication service, and message service using the ports defined in the preceding configuration file. The following CURL requests now show that valid credentials can be exchanged for a JWT and the JWT can be used to access protected resources. We can also show that requests to protected resources are rejected without a valid JWT.

Note that in this example, the message service still doesn't do any authorization of requests. Anyone making an authenticated request could theoretically access anyone else's messages. The message service should be modified to check the user ID from the subject of the JWT and only allow access to messages belonging to that user.

15. We can use `curl` to test registering a new user account:

```
$ curl -X POST -D - http://localhost:8080/auth/register -
d'email=p@eval.ca&password=foobar123&passwordConfirmation=foobar123
'

HTTP/1.1 200
X-Content-Type-Options: nosniff
X-XSS-Protection: 1; mode=block
Cache-Control: no-cache, no-store, max-age=0, must-revalidate
Pragma: no-cache
Expires: 0
X-Frame-Options: DENY
X-Application-Context: application:8080
Date: Mon, 16 Jul 2018 03:27:17 GMT
Content-Type: application/json;charset=UTF-8
Transfer-Encoding: chunked

{"auth_token":"eyJhbGciOiJIUzI1NiJ9.eyJqdGkiOiJmYWQzMGZiMi03MzhmLTR
iM2QtYTIyZC0zZGNmN2NmNGQ1NGIiLCJzdWIiOiJmYWQzMGZiMi03MzhmLTRiM2QtYT
IyZC0zZGNmN2NmNGQ1NGIiLCJpc3MiOiJhdXRoZW50aWNhdGlvbi1zZXJ2aWNlIn0.T
zOKItjBU-AtRMqIB_D1n-qv6IO_zCBIK8ksGzsTC90"}
```

16. Now that we have a JWT, we can include it in the headers of requests to the message service to test that the API Gateway is able to verify and decode the token:

```
$ curl -D - -H "Authorization: Bearer
eyJhbGciOiJIUzI1NiJ9.eyJqdGkiOiI3YmU4N2U3Mi03ZjhhLTQ3ZjktODk3NS1mYz
M5ZTE0NjNmODAiLCJzdWIiOiI3YmU4N2U3Mi03ZjhhLTQ3ZjktODk3NS1mYzM5ZTE0N
jNmODAiLCJpc3MiOiJhdXRoZW50aWNhdGlvbi1zZXJ2aWNlIn0.fpFbHhdSEVKk95m5
Q7iNjkKyM-eHkCGGKchTTKgbGWw" http://localhost:8080/messages/123

HTTP/1.1 404
X-Content-Type-Options: nosniff
X-XSS-Protection: 1; mode=block
Cache-Control: no-cache, no-store, max-age=0, must-revalidate
Pragma: no-cache
Expires: 0
X-Frame-Options: DENY
X-Application-Context: application:8080
```

```
Date: Mon, 16 Jul 2018 04:05:40 GMT
Content-Type: application/json;charset=UTF-8
Transfer-Encoding: chunked

{"timestamp":1532318740403,"status":404,"error":"Not
Found","exception":"com.packtpub.microservices.ch06.message.excepti
ons.MessageNotFoundException","message":"Message 123 could not be
found","path":"/123"}
```

The fact that we get a 404 from the message service shows that the request is getting to that service. If we modify the JWT in the request headers, we should get a 401:

```
$ curl -D - -H "Authorization: Bearer not-the-right-jwt"
http://localhost:8080/messages/123

HTTP/1.1 401
X-Content-Type-Options: nosniff
X-XSS-Protection: 1; mode=block
Cache-Control: no-cache, no-store, max-age=0, must-revalidate
Pragma: no-cache
Expires: 0
X-Frame-Options: DENY
Content-Type: application/json;charset=UTF-8
Transfer-Encoding: chunked
Date: Mon, 23 Jul 2018 04:06:47 GMT

{"timestamp":1532318807874,"status":401,"error":"Unauthorized","mes
sage":"No message available","path":"/messages/123"}
```

Securing containers

The advent of containers has solved many problems for organizations that are managing microservice architectures. Containers allow services to be bundled as a self-contained unit, and the software and its dependencies can be built as a single artifact and then shipped into any environment to be run or scheduled. Instead of relying on complicated configuration-management solutions to manage small changes to production systems, containers support the idea of immutable infrastructure; once the infrastructure is built, it does not have to be upgraded or maintained. Instead, you just build new infrastructure and throw away the old.

Containers also allow organizations to optimize their use of storage and compute resources. Because software can be built as containers, multiple applications can be running on a single virtual machine or piece of hardware, each unaware of the others' existence. While multi-tenancy has many advantages, having multiple services running on the same VM introduces new attack scenarios that a malicious user could exploit. If an attacker is able to exploit a vulnerability in one service, they may be able to use that exploit to attack services running on the same VM. In this kind of setup, by default, the cluster is treated as the security boundary; if you have access to the cluster, you must be trusted.

Depending on the needs of an organization, treating the cluster as the security boundary may not be sufficient and there may be a desire for more security and isolation between containers. The seccomp security facility was introduced into the Linux kernel in Version 2.6.12. It supports restricting the system calls that can be made from a process. Running containerized applications with a seccomp policy essentially sandboxes the service and any other process running in the container. In this recipe, we'll show you how to check that the seccomp is configured in your Linux kernel and demonstrate running a container with a custom seccomp policy.

How to do it...

1. In order to use a seccomp policy with a Docker container, you must be running the container on a host OS with a Linux kernel configured with seccomp support. To check this, you can search for CONFIG_SECCOMP in the kernel configuration file:

```
$ grep CONFIG_SECCOMP= /boot/config-$(uname -r)
CONFIG_SECCOMP=y
```

2. Now that we've verified that seccomp is enabled in the Linux kernel, we can take a look at the default profile that is packaged with Docker (https://github.com/moby/moby/blob/master/profiles/seccomp/default.json). This default policy is sufficient for most needs and is fairly restrictive. If seccomp support is enabled, containers will be run with this policy.

3. To further verify that seccomp is configured and Docker is able to support it, we'll create a simple custom policy and then run a command in a container that demonstrates that the policy is being enforced. Create a file called policy.json:

```
{
    "defaultAction": "SCMP_ACT_ALLOW",
    "syscalls": [
        {
            "name": "chown",
```

```
            "action": "SCMP_ACT_ERRNO"
        }
    ]
}
```

4. Now, run a container executing a shell and try to create a file, then change the ownership. The error message indicates that the container is being restricted by the seccomp policy:

```
$ docker run --rm -it --security-opt seccomp:policy.json busybox
/bin/sh
/ # touch foo
/ # chown root foo
chown: foo: Operation not permitted
```

Secure configuration

Services usually require some form of configuration. A service configuration stores all of the information that could potentially vary depending on the environment the service is deployed in. For example, when running a service locally on a developer's workstation, the service should probably connect to a database that is also running locally. In production, however, the service should connect to the production database. Common data stored in configuration includes the location of and credentials to data stores, access tokens, or other credentials for third-party services and operational information, such as where to send metrics or what values to use when initializing connection pools or configuring timeouts for network connections.

It's important to store configuration separately from code. When you make a configuration change, you should not have to commit a change to a source code repository, create a new build, and run a separate deploy. Ideally, there should be an easy way to change configuration without deploying a new version of a service. Storing configuration in code (for example, hard coding a password in a source code file) is also a bad practice from a security perspective. Anyone with access to the source code has access to the configuration, and in the case of secrets, this is rarely desired. It is a good practice to roll keys and credentials as often as possible, so that even if a secret is compromised or is vulnerable to being compromised, it will not be valid for very long. Hardcoding secrets makes this difficult, which in practice often means it won't happen.

A common best practice is to store configuration in environment variables. This is a good way to expose configuration values to a process in a way that can be changed easily depending on the environment a service is running in. Environment variables are good for non-secret configuration values, such as hostnames, timeouts, and log levels. Environment variables are not sufficient for storing secrets.

Storing secrets as environment variables makes the values accessible to any process running in the same container or process space as the service, which makes them susceptible to being intercepted. There are various solutions for storing secrets separately from the rest of an application's configuration. Applications deployed on a Kubernetes cluster can use a special object type called `secret`, which is intended for this purpose. Kubernetes secrets are encrypted using a private key residing on a master node while in transit between nodes, however, the secret is stored in plaintext at rest. Ideally, secrets should be stored as encrypted values and only decrypted by a process that is explicitly permitted to do so.

Vault is an open source project actively maintained by HashiCorp. Its purpose is to provide an easy-to-use system for storing and accessing secrets securely. In addition to secret-storage, Vault provides access-log auditing, fine-grained access-control, and easy rolling. In this recipe, we'll create a new service, called attachment-service, that is responsible for handling messages' image and video attachments. Attachment-service will use Vault to obtain valid AWS credentials used to access an S3 bucket when uploading photo and video files. The service will also use Vault to obtain database credentials to a MySQL database where attachment metadata will be stored. Non-sensitive configurations, such as the name of the database or the name of the S3 bucket to upload photos and videos to, will be made available to the service as environment variables.

How to do it...

In order to demonstrate using Vault to securely store sensitive configuration data, we'll first create an attachment service that stores sensitive information using environment variables. We'll then integrate Vault so that the same configuration is read from a secure store:

1. Create a new Java project called `attachment-service` with the following `build.gradle` file:

```
group 'com.packtpub.microservices'
version '1.0-SNAPSHOT'

buildscript {
    repositories {
        mavenCentral()
```

```
    }
    dependencies {
        classpath group: 'org.springframework.boot', name: 'spring-
boot-gradle-plugin', version: '1.5.9.RELEASE'
    }
}

apply plugin: 'java'
apply plugin: 'org.springframework.boot'
apply plugin: 'io.spring.dependency-management'

sourceCompatibility = 1.8

repositories {
    mavenCentral()
}

dependencies {
    compile group: 'org.springframework.boot', name: 'spring-boot-
starter-web'
    compile group: 'org.springframework.boot', name: 'spring-boot-
starter-data-jpa', version: '1.5.9.RELEASE'
    compile group: 'mysql', name: 'mysql-connector-java'
    compile group: 'com.amazonaws', name: 'aws-java-sdk-s3',
version: '1.11.375'
    testCompile group: 'junit', name: 'junit', version: '4.12'
}
```

2. Create a new package called
   com.packtpub.microservices.ch06.attachment and create a new class
   called Application, which will serve as our service's entry point. In addition to
   running our Spring Boot application, this class will expose one bean, which is the
   Amazon S3 client. Note that we're using the
   EnvironmentVariableCredentialsProvider class, which reads credentials
   from a set of environment variables for now, this is not what we want to do in
   production:

```java
package com.packtpub.microservices.ch06.attachment;

import com.amazonaws.auth.EnvironmentVariableCredentialsProvider;
import com.amazonaws.regions.Regions;
import com.amazonaws.services.s3.AmazonS3;
import com.amazonaws.services.s3.AmazonS3ClientBuilder;

import org.springframework.boot.SpringApplication;
import
org.springframework.boot.autoconfigure.SpringBootApplication;
```

```
import org.springframework.context.annotation.Bean;

@SpringBootApplication
public class Application {

    @Bean
    public AmazonS3 getS3Client() {
        AmazonS3ClientBuilder client =
AmazonS3ClientBuilder.standard();
        return client.withCredentials(
                new
EnvironmentVariableCredentialsProvider()).withRegion(Regions.US_WES
T_2).build();
    }

    public static void main(String[] args) {
        SpringApplication.run(Application.class, args);
    }
}
```

3. Create a new package called
   `com.packtpub.microservices.ch06.attachment.models` and a new class
   called `Attachment`. This will be the representation of attachments that we store
   in a relational database:

```
package com.packtpub.microservices.ch06.attachment.models;

import org.hibernate.annotations.GenericGenerator;

import javax.persistence.Column;
import javax.persistence.Entity;
import javax.persistence.GeneratedValue;
import javax.persistence.Id;

@Entity
public class Attachment {

    @Id
    @GeneratedValue(generator = "uuid")
    @GenericGenerator(name = "uuid", strategy = "uuid2")
    private String id;

    @Column(unique = true)
    private String messageId;
    private String url;
    private String fileName;
    private Integer mediaType;
```

```java
    public Attachment(String messageId, String url, String
fileName, Integer mediaType) {
        this.messageId = messageId;
        this.url = url;
        this.fileName = fileName;
        this.mediaType = mediaType;
    }

    public String getId() {
        return id;
    }

    public void setId(String id) {
        this.id = id;
    }

    public String getMessageId() {
        return messageId;
    }

    public void setMessageId(String messageId) {
        this.messageId = messageId;
    }

    public String getUrl() {
        return url;
    }

    public void setUrl(String url) {
        this.url = url;
    }

    public String getFileName() {
        return fileName;
    }

    public void setFileName(String fileName) {
        this.fileName = fileName;
    }

    public Integer getMediaType() {
        return mediaType;
    }

    public void setMediaType(Integer mediaType) {
        this.mediaType = mediaType;
    }
}
```

4. In order to perform basic operations on the previously defined `Attachment` class, we'll create a new package called `com.packtpub.microservices.ch06.attachment.data` and an interface called `AttachmentRepository`, which extends `CrudRepository`. We'll also define one custom method signature that allows a caller to find all attachments related to a specific message:

```
package com.packtpub.microservices.ch06.attachment.data;

import
com.packtpub.microservices.ch06.attachment.models.Attachment;
import org.springframework.data.repository.CrudRepository;

import java.util.List;

public interface AttachmentRepository extends
CrudRepository<Attachment, String> {
    public List<Attachment> findByMessageId(String messageId);
}
```

5. We also need a way to model incoming requests. Our service will accept requests as JSON sent in the request body. The JSON object will have a file name and contain the file data as a Base64-encoded string. Create a new class called `AttachmentRequest` with the following definition:

```
package com.packtpub.microservices.ch06.attachment.models;

import com.fasterxml.jackson.annotation.JsonProperty;

import java.util.Map;

public class AttachmentRequest {
    private String fileName;

    private String data;

    public AttachmentRequest() {}

    public AttachmentRequest(String fileName, String data) {
        this.fileName = fileName;
        this.data = data;
    }

    public String getFileName() {
        return fileName;
    }
```

```
        public void setFileName(String fileName) {
            this.fileName = fileName;
        }

        public String getData() {
            return data;
        }

        public void setData(String data) {
            this.data = data;
        }

        @JsonProperty("file")
        private void unpackFileName(Map<String, String> file) {
            this.fileName = file.get("name");
            this.data = file.get("data");
        }
    }
```

6. In our controller, which we'll define next, we'll need to return an HTTP 404 response to callers if no attachments can be found for a particular message. In order to do this, create a new package called com.packtpub.microservices.ch06.attachment.exceptions and a new class called AttachmentNotFoundException:

```
package com.packtpub.microservices.ch06.attachment.exceptions;

import org.springframework.http.HttpStatus;
import org.springframework.web.bind.annotation.ResponseStatus;

@ResponseStatus(code = HttpStatus.NOT_FOUND, reason = "No
attachment(s) found")
public class AttachmentNotFoundException extends RuntimeException
{}
```

7. We'll put everything together in our controller. In this basic example, two methods are defined; one that lists attachments for a specific message and one that creates a new attachment. The attachment is uploaded to an Amazon S3 bucket, the name of which is specified in a configuration value. Create a new package called com.packtpub.microservices.ch06.attachment.controllers and a new class called AttachmentController:

```
package com.packtpub.microservices.ch06.attachment.controllers;

import com.amazonaws.services.s3.AmazonS3;
```

```
import com.amazonaws.services.s3.model.CannedAccessControlList;
import com.amazonaws.services.s3.model.ObjectMetadata;
import com.amazonaws.services.s3.model.PutObjectRequest;
import
com.packtpub.microservices.ch06.attachment.data.AttachmentRepositor
y;
import
com.packtpub.microservices.ch06.attachment.exceptions.AttachmentNot
FoundException;
import
com.packtpub.microservices.ch06.attachment.models.Attachment;
import
com.packtpub.microservices.ch06.attachment.models.AttachmentRequest
;
import org.apache.commons.codec.binary.Base64;
import org.springframework.beans.factory.annotation.Autowired;
import org.springframework.beans.factory.annotation.Value;
import org.springframework.web.bind.annotation.*;

import java.io.ByteArrayInputStream;
import java.io.InputStream;
import java.util.List;

@RestController
public class AttachmentController {

    @Autowired
    private AttachmentRepository attachmentRepository;

    @Autowired
    private AmazonS3 s3Client;

    @Value("${s3.bucket-name}")
    private String bucketName;

    @RequestMapping(path = "/message/{message_id}/attachments",
method = RequestMethod.GET, produces = "application/json")
    public List<Attachment>
getAttachments(@PathVariable("message_id") String messageId) {
        List<Attachment> attachments =
attachmentRepository.findByMessageId(messageId);
        if (attachments.isEmpty()) {
            throw new AttachmentNotFoundException();
        }
        return attachments;
    }

    @RequestMapping(path = "/message/{message_id}/attachments",
```

```
method = RequestMethod.POST, produces = "application/json")
    public Attachment create(@PathVariable("message_id") String
messageId, @RequestBody AttachmentRequest request) {

        byte[] byteArray = Base64.decodeBase64(request.getData());

        ObjectMetadata metadata = new ObjectMetadata();
        metadata.setContentLength(byteArray.length);
        metadata.setContentType("image/jpeg");
        metadata.setCacheControl("public, max-age=31536000");
        InputStream stream = new ByteArrayInputStream(byteArray);

        String fullyResolved = String.format("%s/%s", messageId,
request.getFileName());

        s3Client.putObject(
            new PutObjectRequest(bucketName, fullyResolved, stream,
metadata)
        .withCannedAcl(CannedAccessControlList.PublicRead));

        String url =
String.format("https://%s.s3.amazonaws.com/%s", bucketName,
fullyResolved);

        Attachment attachment = new Attachment(messageId, url,
request.getFileName(), 1);
        attachmentRepository.save(attachment);
        return attachment;
    }
}
```

8. In order for any of this to work, we have to create a properties file. Java properties files support a syntax for getting values from environment variables, which is shown in the following code. Create a new file in the `src/main/resources` directory called `application.yml`:

```
spring:
  jpa.hibernate.ddl-auto: create
  datasource.url: ${DATABASE_URL}
  datasource.username: ${DATABASE_USERNAME}
  datasource.password: ${DATABASE_PASSWORD}

s3:
  bucket-name: ${BUCKET_NAME}
```

This example works well enough. `EnvironmentVariableCredentialsProvider` in the AWS SDK expects `AWS_ACCESS_KEY_ID` and `AWS_SECRET_ACCESS_KEY` to be set, and we specify that a number of non-sensitive configuration values should be similarly read from environment variables. This is clearly better than hardcoding configuration values, but we're still exposing secrets to any process running in the same container or process space as our service. The environment variables also have to be set somewhere (by a configuration management system or specified in a Dockerfile), so we haven't solved the problem of storing sensitive secrets. Next, we'll modify our new service to read S3 credentials from Vault.

 In this recipe, we'll be running Vault in development mode. Installing Vault for production use is a big topic that cannot be properly covered in a single recipe. For the production use of Vault, please consult the excellent documentation available at `https://www.vaultproject.io/intro/index.html`.

9. Install `vault` on your local development machine. See `http://www.vaultproject.io` for instructions for any platform. If you are running macOS X and use **HomeBrew**, you can install Vault with a single command:

   ```
   $ brew install vault
   ```

10. Run the `vault server` in development mode, providing a simple-to-remember root token:

    ```
    $ vault server --dev --dev-root-token-
    id="00000000-0000-0000-0000-000000000000"
    ```

11. Enable a new instance of a `kv` secrets engine with a path specific to this service:

    ```
    $ vault secrets enable –path=secret/attachment-service
    ```

12. Write the AWS access key and secret pair to `vault` as secrets. Substitute the placeholders for your actual AWS access key ID and AWS secret access key:

    ```
    $ vault write secret/attachment-service
    attachment.awsAccessKeyId=<access-key>
    attachment.awsSecretAccessKey=<access-secret>
    ```

13. In order for our service to read these values from Vault, we'll use a library that simplifies Vault integration for Spring Boot applications. Modify our project's `build.gradle` file and add the following dependency:

```
group 'com.packtpub.microservices'
version '1.0-SNAPSHOT'

buildscript {
    repositories {
        mavenCentral()
    }
    dependencies {
        classpath group: 'org.springframework.boot', name: 'spring-
boot-gradle-plugin', version: '1.5.9.RELEASE'
    }
}

apply plugin: 'java'
apply plugin: 'org.springframework.boot'
apply plugin: 'io.spring.dependency-management'

sourceCompatibility = 1.8

repositories {
    mavenCentral()
}

dependencies {
    compile group: 'org.springframework.boot', name: 'spring-boot-
starter-web'
    compile group: 'org.springframework.boot', name: 'spring-boot-
starter-data-jpa', version: '1.5.9.RELEASE'
    compile group: 'org.springframework.cloud', name: 'spring-
cloud-starter-vault-config', version: '1.1.1.RELEASE'
    compile group: 'mysql', name: 'mysql-connector-java'
    compile group: 'com.amazonaws', name: 'aws-java-sdk-s3',
version: '1.11.375'
    testCompile group: 'junit', name: 'junit', version: '4.12'
}
```

14. Our application needs a configuration class to store values read from Vault.
Create a new package called
com.packtpub.microservices.ch06.attachment.config and a new class
called Configuration:

```
package com.packtpub.microservices.ch06.attachment.config;

import
org.springframework.boot.context.properties.ConfigurationProperties
;

@ConfigurationProperties("attachment")
public class Configuration {

    private String awsAccessKeyId;

    private String awsSecretAccessKey;

    public String getAwsAccessKeyId() {
        return awsAccessKeyId;
    }

    public void setAwsAccessKeyId(String awsAccessKeyId) {
        this.awsAccessKeyId = awsAccessKeyId;
    }

    public String getAwsSecretAccessKey() {
        return awsSecretAccessKey;
    }

    public void setAwsSecretAccessKey(String awsSecretAccessKey) {
        this.awsSecretAccessKey = awsSecretAccessKey;
    }
}
```

15. Modify the Application class to create an instance of the class we just created.
Then use the instance when creating the S3 client so that we can use credentials
taken from Vault instead of environment variables:

```
package com.packtpub.microservices.ch06.attachment;

import com.amazonaws.auth.AWSCredentials;
import com.amazonaws.auth.AWSStaticCredentialsProvider;
import com.amazonaws.auth.BasicAWSCredentials;
import com.amazonaws.regions.Regions;
import com.amazonaws.services.s3.AmazonS3;
import com.amazonaws.services.s3.AmazonS3ClientBuilder;
```

```
import
com.packtpub.microservices.ch06.attachment.config.Configuration;
import org.springframework.boot.SpringApplication;
import
org.springframework.boot.autoconfigure.SpringBootApplication;
import
org.springframework.boot.context.properties.EnableConfigurationProp
erties;
import org.springframework.context.annotation.Bean;

@SpringBootApplication
@EnableConfigurationProperties(Configuration.class)
public class Application {

    private final Configuration config;

    public Application(Configuration config) {
        this.config = config;
    }

    @Bean
    public AmazonS3 getS3Client() {
        AmazonS3ClientBuilder client =
AmazonS3ClientBuilder.standard();
        AWSCredentials credentials = new
BasicAWSCredentials(config.getAwsAccessKeyId(),
config.getAwsSecretAccessKey());
        return client.withCredentials(
                new
AWSStaticCredentialsProvider(credentials)).withRegion(Regions.US_WE
ST_2).build();
    }

    public static void main(String[] args) {
        SpringApplication.run(Application.class, args);
    }
}
```

That's it! The attachment service is now configured to read AWS credentials from Vault.

Secure logging

Together with traces and metrics, logs are an essential component of an observable system (we'll discuss Observability more generally in `Chapter 7`, *Monitoring and Observability*). Logs are an ordered, timestamped sequence of events that originated in a particular system.

In a microservice architecture, the increased complexity of having multiple services makes having good logs essential. The exact criteria that makes logs good is subjective, but generally speaking, good logs should help an engineer piece together events that may have led to a specific error state or bug. Logs are usually organized by levels, a configurable toggle that allows a developer to instruct a service to be more or less verbose with the information sent to logs.

While essential for observing the behavior of systems in production, logs can also present privacy and security risks. Having too much information sent from systems to logs can give a would-be attacker information about users of your system, or sensitive information such as tokens or keys that can be used to attack other parts of your system. Having a microservice architecture spreads out this possible attack surface, making it even more important to have a carefully planned strategy for how your services should log information.

Infrastructure as Code

Microservices architectures typically require more frequent provisioning of compute resources. Having more nodes in a system increases the attack surface that an attacker could scan for possible vulnerabilities. One of the easiest ways to leave a system vulnerable is to lose track of the inventory and leave multiple, heterogeneous configurations active. Before configuration-management systems, such as, Puppet or Ansible were popular, it was common to have a set of custom shell scripts that would *bootstrap* new servers in a system. This worked well enough, but as the needs of the system grew, and the shell scripts were modified, it became unwieldy to bring older parts of the system up to date with the changing standards. This type of configuration drift would often leave legacy parts of a system vulnerable to attack. Configuration-management solved many of these problems by allowing teams to use code, usually with a declarative syntax, to describe how nodes in a system should be configured. Configuration-management systems typically did not deal with provisioning actual compute resources, such as compute nodes, data stores, or network storage.

Infrastructure as Code is the process of managing infrastructure-provisioning and maintenance through machine-readable code files rather than manually. Using code to describe the infrastructure allows for effective versioning, reviews, and rollbacks of changes to a system. Being able to automate the process of bringing up a database node or adding a compute node to a cluster frees developers up to worry about their applications, relatively assured that they are not leaving old configurations out in the wild. Together with immutable infrastructure, Infrastructure as Code provides an additional safety net against a system being compromised by vulnerable, forgotten components.

In this recipe, we'll demonstrate using *Terraform*, an open source tool created by HashiCorp, to provision a collection of AWS resources, including an EC2 instance and a Redis ElastiCache. We'll guarantee that resources provisioned with Terraform share configurations with regards to network access, backups, and other security considerations.

How to do it...

1. Before using terraform, you'll have to install it. Instructions are available on the project site, but if you are running macOS X and use HomeBrew (https:// brew.sh/), you can issue the following command:

   ```
   $ brew install terraform
   ```

2. Create a new file called example.tf. This will contain configuration for our EC2 instance and ElastiCache instance. We'll use a default **Amazon Machine Image** (**AMI**) and enable daily snapshots that will be kept for five days:

   ```
   provider "aws" {
       access_key = "ACCESS_KEY"
       secret_key = "SECRET_KEY"
       region = "us-east-1"
   }

   resource "aws_instance" "example" {
     ami           = "ami-b374d5a5"
     instance_type = "t2.micro"
   }

   resource "aws_elasticache_cluster" "example" {
     cluster_id           = "cluster-example"
     engine               = "redis"
     node_type            = "cache.m3.medium"
     num_cache_nodes      = 1
     parameter_group_name = "default.redis3.2"
     port                 = 6379
     snapshot_window      = "05:00-09:00"
     snapshot_retention_limit = 5
   }
   ```

   Replace ACCESS_KEY and SECRET_KEY with a valid AWS access key pair.

3. Initialize terraform. This will install the AWS provider referenced in the preceding file:

```
$ terraform init
```

4. Terraform works by presenting an execution plan and then asking whether you'd like to proceed by applying the plan. Run the following command and type yes when prompted:

```
$ terraform apply

aws_instance.example: Refreshing state... (ID: i-09b5cf5ed923d60f4)
```

An execution plan has been generated and is shown in the following code. Resource actions are indicated with the following symbols: + create.

Terraform will perform the following actions:

```
+ aws_elasticache_cluster.example
      id: <computed>
      apply_immediately: <computed>
      availability_zone: <computed>
      az_mode: <computed>
      cache_nodes.#: <computed>
      cluster_address: <computed>
      cluster_id: "cluster-example"
      configuration_endpoint: <computed>
      engine: "redis"
      engine_version: <computed>
      maintenance_window: <computed>
      node_type: "cache.m3.medium"
      num_cache_nodes: "1"
      parameter_group_name: <computed>
      port: "6379"
      replication_group_id: <computed>
      security_group_ids.#: <computed>
      security_group_names.#: <computed>
      snapshot_retention_limit: "5"
      snapshot_window: "05:00-09:00"
      subnet_group_name: <computed>


Plan: 1 to add, 0 to change, 0 to destroy.
Do you want to perform these actions?
```

Terraform will perform the actions described earlier. Only `yes` will be accepted to approve:

```
Enter a value: yes
```

. . .

5. Log into your AWS management console and you'll see that a new Redis cluster and EC2 instance have been created. Terraform can also help you clean up. In order to destroy these two resources, run the destroy command and type in `yes` when prompted:

```
$ terraform destroy
```

Terraform is an incredibly powerful tool. In this recipe, we used it to create a single EC2 instance and an ElastiCache Cluster instance. You can do loads more with Terraform – the subject of Infrastructure as Code could fill a cookbook of its own. Thankfully, the docs provided by HashiCorp (`https://www.terraform.io/docs/index.html`) are excellent and I would recommend reading them.

Using an Infrastructure as Code solution will make provisioning and managing resources a much safer process, limiting the possibility of losing track of legacy infrastructure with out-of-date configurations.

Monitoring and Observability 7

In this chapter, we will cover the following recipes:

- Structured JSON logging
- Collecting metrics with StatsD and Graphite
- Collecting metrics with Prometheus
- Making debugging easier with tracing
- Alerting when something goes wrong

Introduction

Microservices add complexity to an architecture. With more moving parts in a system, monitoring and observing the behavior of the system becomes more important and more challenging. In a microservice architecture, failure conditions impacting one service can cascade in unexpected ways, impacting the system as a whole. A faulty switch somewhere in a datacenter may be causing unusually high latency for a service, perhaps resulting in intermittent timeouts in requests originating from the API Gateway, which may result in unexpected user impact, which results in an alert being fired. This kind of scenario is not uncommon in a microservice architecture and requires forethought so that engineers can easily determine the nature of customer-impacting incidents. Distributed systems are bound to experience certain failures and special consideration must be taken to build observability into systems.

Another shift that microservices have necessitated is the move to DevOps. Many traditional monitoring solutions were developed at a time when operations were the sole responsibility of a special and distinct group of system administrators or operations engineers. System administrators and operations engineers are often interested in system-level or host-level metrics, such as CPU, memory disk, and network usage. These metrics are important but only make up a small part of observability. **Observability** must also be considered by engineers writing microservices. It's equally important to use metrics to be able to observe events unique to a system, such as certain types of exceptions being thrown or the number of events emitted to a queue.

Planning for observability also gives us the information we need to effectively test systems in production. Ephemeral environments for staging and integration testing can be useful, but there are entire classes of failure states that they are unable to test for. As discussed in Chapter 5, *Reliability Patterns*, Gamedays and other forms of failure injection are critical for improving the resilience of systems. Observable systems lend themselves to this kind of testing, allowing engineers to gain confidence in our understanding of the system.

In this chapter, we'll introduce several tenants of monitoring and observability. We'll demonstrate how to modify our services to emit structured logs. We'll also take a look at metrics, using a number of different systems for collecting, aggregating, and visualizing metrics. Finally we'll look at tracing, a way to look at requests as they travel through various components of a system and alert us when user-impacting error conditions are detected.

Structured JSON logging

Outputting useful logs is a key part of building an observable service. What constitutes a useful log is subjective, but a good set of guidelines is that logs should contain timestamped information about key events in a system. A good logging system supports the notion of configurable log levels, so the amount of information sent to logs can be dialed up or down for a specific amount of time depending on the needs of engineers working with the system. For example, when testing a service against failure scenarios in production, it may be useful to turn up the log level and get more detail about events in the system.

The two most popular logging libraries for Java applications are **Log4j** (`https://logging.apache.org/log4j/2.x/`) and **Logback** (`https://logback.qos.ch/`). By default, both of these libraries will emit log entries in an unstructured format, usually space-separated fields including information such as a timestamp, log level, and message. This is useful, but especially so in a microservices architecture, where multiple services are emitting event logs possibly to a centralized log store; it's extremely useful to emit structured logs with some consistency.

JSON has become a common standard for passing messages between systems. Nearly every popular language has libraries for parsing and generating JSON. It's lightweight, yet structured, making it a good choice for data, such as event logs. Emitting event logs in JSON makes it easier to feed your service's logs into a centralized store and have log data analyzed and queried.

In this recipe, we'll modify our message-service to emit logs using the popular `logback` library for Java applications.

How to do it...

Let's have a look at the following steps:

1. Open the message-service project from `Chapter 6`, *Security*. The first change we'll make is to add the `logback` library to the `build.gradle` file:

```
group 'com.packtpub.microservices'
version '1.0-SNAPSHOT'

buildscript {
    repositories {
        mavenCentral()
    }
    dependencies {
        classpath group: 'org.springframework.boot', name: 'spring-boot-gradle-plugin', version: '1.5.9.RELEASE'
    }
}

apply plugin: 'java'
apply plugin: 'org.springframework.boot'

sourceCompatibility = 1.8

repositories {
    mavenCentral()
```

```
    }

    dependencies {
        compile group: 'org.springframework.boot', name: 'spring-boot-
    starter-web'
        compile group: 'io.github.resilience4j', name: 'resilience4j-
    circuitbreaker', version: '0.11.0'
        compile group: 'net.logstash.logback', name: 'logstash-logback-
    encoder', version: '4.7'
        testCompile group: 'junit', name: 'junit', version: '4.12'
    }
```

2. Create a `logback.xml` configuration file. In the configuration file, we'll create a single logger, called `jsonLogger`, that references a single appender, called `consoleAppender`:

```
<?xml version="1.0" encoding="utf-8"?>
<configuration>
    <appender name="consoleAppender"
class="ch.qos.logback.core.ConsoleAppender">
        <encoder
class="net.logstash.logback.encoder.LogstashEncoder"/>
    </appender>
    <logger name="jsonLogger" additivity="false" level="DEBUG">
        <appender-ref ref="consoleAppender"/>
    </logger>
    <root level="INFO">
        <appender-ref ref="consoleAppender"/>
    </root>
</configuration>
```

3. Add a single sample log message to `Application.java` to test our new logging configuration:

```
package com.packtpub.microservices.ch07.message;

import
com.packtpub.microservices.ch07.message.clients.SocialGraphClient;
import org.apache.log4j.LogManager;
import org.apache.log4j.Logger;
import org.springframework.boot.SpringApplication;
import
org.springframework.boot.autoconfigure.SpringBootApplication;
import org.springframework.context.annotation.Bean;
import org.springframework.scheduling.annotation.EnableAsync;
import
org.springframework.scheduling.concurrent.ThreadPoolTaskExecutor;
```

```
import java.util.concurrent.Executor;

@SpringBootApplication
@EnableAsync
public class Application {

    private Logger logger =
LogManager.getLogger(Application.class);

    @Bean
    public MessageRepository messageRepository() {
        return new MessageRepository();
    }

    @Bean
    public SocialGraphClient socialGraphClient() {
        return new SocialGraphClient("http://localhost:4567");
    }

    public static void main(String[] args) {
        logger.info("Starting application");
        SpringApplication.run(Application.class, args);
    }

    @Bean
    public Executor asyncExecutor() {
        ThreadPoolTaskExecutor executor = new
ThreadPoolTaskExecutor();
        executor.setCorePoolSize(2);
        executor.setMaxPoolSize(2);
        executor.setQueueCapacity(500);
        executor.setThreadNamePrefix("SocialServiceCall-");
        executor.initialize();
        return executor;
    }
}
```

4. Run the application and see that log messages are now emitted in JSON:

```
$ ./gradlew bootRun

> Task :bootRun
{"@timestamp":"2018-08-09T22:08:22.959-05:00","@version":1,"message
":"Starting
application","logger_name":"com.packtpub.microservices.ch07.message
.Application","thread_name":"main","level":"INFO","level_value":200
00}
```

```
      .   ____          _            __ _ _
     /\\ / ___'_ __ _ _(_)_ __  __ _ \ \ \ \
    ( ( )\___ | '_ | '_| | '_ \/ _` | \ \ \ \
     \\/  ___)| |_)| | | | | || (_| |  ) ) ) )
      '  |____| .__|_| |_|_| |_\__, | / / / /
     =========|_|==============|___/=/_/_/_/
     :: Spring Boot ::        (v1.5.9.RELEASE)
```

{"@timestamp":"2018-08-09T22:08:23.786-05:00","@version":1,"message":"Starting Application on fartlek.local with PID 82453 (/Users/posman/projects/microservices-cookbook/chapter07/message-service/build/classes/java/main started by posman in /Users/posman/projects/microservices-cookbook/chapter07/message-service)","logger_name":"com.packtpub.microservices.ch07.message.Application","thread_name":"main","level":"INFO","level_value":20000}

Collecting metrics with StatsD and Graphite

Metrics are numeric measurements over time. The most common types of metrics collected in our systems are counters, timers, and gauges. A counter is exactly what it sounds like, a value that is incremented a number of times over some time period. A timer can be used to measure recurring events in a system, such as the amount of time it takes to serve a request or perform a database query. Gauges are just arbitrary numeric values that can be recorded.

StatsD is an open source network daemon invented in 2011 at Etsy. Metrics data is pushed to a `statsd` server, often on the same server, which aggregates data before sending it on to a durable backend. One of the most common backends used with `statsd` is **Graphite**, an open source time-series storage engine and graphing tool. Together, Graphite and StatsD make up a very popular metrics stack. They're easy to get started with and enjoy large communities and a large selection of tools and libraries.

Spring Boot has a sub-project called **Actuator** that adds a number of production readiness features to a service. Actuator gives us our services certain metrics for free, together with a project called micrometer, Actuator enables a vendor-neutral API to various metric's backends. We'll use Actuator and micrometer in this recipe and the next one.

In this recipe, we'll add Actuator to the message-service we've worked with in previous recipes. We'll create a few custom metrics and demonstrate using `statsd` and `graphite` to graph metrics from our application. We'll run `statsd` and `graphite` locally in docker containers.

How to do it...

Let's look at the following steps:

1. Open the message-service project from previous recipes. We're going to upgrade the version of Spring Boot and add `actuator` and `micrometer` to our list of dependencies. Modify the `build.gradle` file to look like the following:

```
group 'com.packtpub.microservices'
version '1.0-SNAPSHOT'

buildscript {
    repositories {
        mavenCentral()
    }
    dependencies {
        classpath group: 'org.springframework.boot', name: 'spring-
boot-gradle-plugin', version: '2.0.4.RELEASE'
    }
}

apply plugin: 'java'
apply plugin: 'org.springframework.boot'

sourceCompatibility = 1.8

repositories {
    mavenCentral()
}

dependencies {
    compile group: 'org.springframework.boot', name: 'spring-boot-
starter-web', version: '2.0.4.RELEASE'
    compile group: 'org.springframework.boot', name: 'spring-boot-
starter-actuator', version: '2.0.4.RELEASE'
    compile group: 'io.micrometer', name: 'micrometer-core',
version: '1.0.6'
    compile group: 'io.micrometer', name: 'micrometer-registry-
statsd', version: '1.0.6'
    compile group: 'io.github.resilience4j', name: 'resilience4j-
circuitbreaker', version: '0.11.0'
    compile group: 'log4j', name: 'log4j', version: '1.2.17'
    compile group: 'net.logstash.logback', name: 'logstash-logback-
encoder', version: '5.2'
    testCompile group: 'junit', name: 'junit', version: '4.12'
}
```

2. Open `application.yml` in the `src/main/resources` directory and add the following:

```
server:
  port:
    8082

management:
  metrics:
    export:
      statsd:
        enabled: true
        flavor: "etsy"
        host:
          0.0.0.0
        port:
          8125
```

3. Our application now supports emitting metrics to a locally-running instance of `statsd`. Open `MessageController.java` and add the `Timed` annotation to the class as well as the `get` method:

```
package com.packtpub.microservices.ch07.message.controllers;

import com.packtpub.microservices.ch07.message.MessageRepository;
import
com.packtpub.microservices.ch07.message.clients.SocialGraphClient;
import
com.packtpub.microservices.ch07.message.exceptions.MessageNotFoundE
xception;
import
com.packtpub.microservices.ch07.message.exceptions.MessageSendForbi
ddenException;
import com.packtpub.microservices.ch07.message.models.Message;
import
com.packtpub.microservices.ch07.message.models.UserFriendships;
import io.micrometer.core.annotation.Timed;
import io.micrometer.statsd.StatsdMeterRegistry;
import org.springframework.beans.factory.annotation.Autowired;
import org.springframework.http.ResponseEntity;
import org.springframework.scheduling.annotation.Async;
import org.springframework.web.bind.annotation.*;
import org.springframework.web.client.RestTemplate;
import
org.springframework.web.servlet.support.ServletUriComponentsBuilder
;
```

```java
import java.net.URI;
import java.util.List;
import java.util.concurrent.CompletableFuture;

@RestController
@Timed
public class MessageController {

    @Autowired
    private MessageRepository messagesStore;

    @Autowired
    private SocialGraphClient socialGraphClient;

    @Autowired
    private StatsdMeterRegistry registry;

    @Timed(value="get.messages")
    @RequestMapping(path = "/{id}", method = RequestMethod.GET,
produces = "application/json")
    public Message get(@PathVariable("id") String id) throws
MessageNotFoundException {
        registry.counter("get_messages").increment();
        return messagesStore.get(id);
    }

    @RequestMapping(path = "/", method = RequestMethod.POST,
produces = "application/json")
    public ResponseEntity<Message> send(@RequestBody Message
message) throws MessageSendForbiddenException {

        List<String> friendships =
socialGraphClient.getFriendships(message.getSender());
        if (!friendships.contains(message.getRecipient())) {
            throw new MessageSendForbiddenException("Must be
friends to send message");
        }

        Message saved = messagesStore.save(message);
        URI location = ServletUriComponentsBuilder
                .fromCurrentRequest().path("/{id}")
                .buildAndExpand(saved.getId()).toUri();
        return ResponseEntity.created(location).build();
    }

    @Async
    public CompletableFuture<Boolean> isFollowing(String fromUser,
String toUser) {
```

```
            String url = String.format(
    "http://localhost:4567/followings?user=%s&filter=%s",
                    fromUser, toUser);

        RestTemplate template = new RestTemplate();
        UserFriendships followings = template.getForObject(url,
    UserFriendships.class);

        return CompletableFuture.completedFuture(
                followings.getFriendships().isEmpty()
        );
    }
}
```

4. In order to demonstrate that metrics are actually being emitted, we'll run `statsd` and graphite locally in a docker container. Having installed `docker`, run the following command, which will pull down an image from `dockerhub` and run a container locally:

```
docker run -d --name graphite --restart=always \
  -p 80:80 -p 2003-2004:2003-2004 -p 2023-2024:2023-2024 \
  -p 8125:8125/udp -p 8126:8126 \
  hopsoft/graphite-statsd
```

5. Now, visit `http://localhost` to see your metrics!

Collecting metrics with Prometheus

Prometheus is an open source monitoring and alerting toolkit originally developed in 2012 at **SoundCloud**. It was inspired by Borgmon at Google. In contrast to the push model employed by systems such as `statsd`, Prometheus uses a pull model for collecting metrics. Instead of each service being responsible for pushing metrics to a `statsd` server, Prometheus is responsible for scraping an endpoint exposed by services that have metrics. This inversion of responsibilities provides some benefits when operating metrics at scale. Targets in Prometheus can be configured manually or via service discovery.

In contrast to the hierarchical format that systems such as Graphite use to store metrics data, Prometheus employs a multidimensional data model. Time-series data in Prometheus is identified by a metric name (such as `http_request_duration_seconds`) and one or more labels (such as `service=message-service` and `method=POST`). This format can make it easier to standardize metrics across a number of different applications, which is particularly valuable in a microservices architecture.

In this recipe, we'll continue to use message-service and the Actuator and micrometer libraries. We'll configure micrometer to use the Prometheus metrics registry and we'll expose an endpoint that Prometheus can scrape in order to collect metrics from our service. We'll then configure Prometheus to scrape the message-service (running locally) and run Prometheus locally to verify that we can query our metrics.

How to do it...

1. Open the message-service and edit `build.gradle` to include actuator and the micrometer-prometheus dependencies:

```
group 'com.packtpub.microservices'
version '1.0-SNAPSHOT'

buildscript {
    repositories {
        mavenCentral()
    }
    dependencies {
        classpath group: 'org.springframework.boot', name: 'spring-
boot-gradle-plugin', version: '2.0.4.RELEASE'
    }
}

apply plugin: 'java'
apply plugin: 'org.springframework.boot'

sourceCompatibility = 1.8

repositories {
    mavenCentral()
}

dependencies {
    compile group: 'org.springframework.boot', name: 'spring-boot-
starter-web', version: '2.0.4.RELEASE'
    compile group: 'org.springframework.boot', name: 'spring-boot-
starter-actuator', version: '2.0.4.RELEASE'
    compile group: 'io.micrometer', name: 'micrometer-core',
version: '1.0.6'
    compile group: 'io.micrometer', name: 'micrometer-registry-
prometheus', version: '1.0.6'
    compile group: 'io.github.resilience4j', name: 'resilience4j-
circuitbreaker', version: '0.11.0'
    compile group: 'log4j', name: 'log4j', version: '1.2.17'
```

```
    compile group: 'net.logstash.logback', name: 'logstash-logback-
encoder', version: '5.2'
    testCompile group: 'junit', name: 'junit', version: '4.12'
}
```

2. Add the following to `application.yml`. This will enable an endpoint that exposes metrics collected in the Prometheus metrics registry. Notice that we're opening another port for the management endpoints added by `actuator`:

```
server:
  port:
    8082

management:
  server:
    port:
      8081
  endpoint:
    metrics:
      enabled: true
    prometheus:
      enabled: true
  endpoints:
    web:
      base-path: "/manage"
      exposure:
        include: "*"
  metrics:
    export:
      prometheus:
        enabled: true
```

3. We can now test that our service is exposing metrics on the `/manage/prometheus` endpoint. Run the service and make the following `curl` request:

```
$ curl http://localhost:8081/manage/prometheus

# HELP tomcat_global_request_seconds
# TYPE tomcat_global_request_seconds summary
tomcat_global_request_seconds_count{name="http-nio-8082",} 0.0
tomcat_global_request_seconds_sum{name="http-nio-8082",} 0.0
# HELP tomcat_sessions_active_max
# TYPE tomcat_sessions_active_max gauge
tomcat_sessions_active_max 0.0
# HELP process_uptime_seconds The uptime of the Java virtual
machine
```

```
# TYPE process_uptime_seconds gauge
process_uptime_seconds 957.132
# HELP jvm_gc_live_data_size_bytes Size of old generation memory
pool after a full GC
# TYPE jvm_gc_live_data_size_bytes gauge
jvm_gc_live_data_size_bytes 1.9244032E7
```

4. Configure and run Prometheus in a docker container. Create a new file in the /tmp directory, called prometheus.yml, with information about our target:

```
# my global config
global:
  scrape_interval: 15s # Set the scrape interval to every 15
seconds. Default is every 1 minute.
  evaluation_interval: 15s # Evaluate rules every 15 seconds. The
default is every 1 minute.
  # scrape_timeout is set to the global default (10s).

# Alertmanager configuration
alerting:
  alertmanagers:
  - static_configs:
    - targets:
      # - alertmanager:9093

# Load rules once and periodically evaluate them according to the
global 'evaluation_interval'.
rule_files:
  # - "first_rules.yml"
  # - "second_rules.yml"

# A scrape configuration containing exactly one endpoint to scrape:
# Here it's Prometheus itself.
scrape_configs:
  # The job name is added as a label `job=<job_name>` to any
timeseries scraped from this config.
  - job_name: 'prometheus'

    # metrics_path defaults to '/metrics'
    # scheme defaults to 'http'.

    static_configs:
    - targets: ['localhost:9090']

  - job_name: 'message-service'
    metrics_path: '/manage/prometheus'
    static_configs:
    - targets: ['localhost:8081']
```

5. Download and extract the version of Prometheus for your platform. Instructions are on the Prometheus website (`https://prometheus.io/docs/introduction/first_steps/`). Run Prometheus with the configuration file we created in the previous step:

```
$ ./prometheus --config.file=/tmp/prometheus.yml
```

6. Open `http://localhost:9090` in your browser to issue Prometheus queries and see your metrics! Until you start making requests to your service, the only metrics you'll see will be the JVM and system metrics, but this should give you an idea of the kind of querying you can do with Prometheus and demonstrate how the scraper works.

Making debugging easier with tracing

In a microservices architecture, a single request can go through several different services and result in writes to several different data stores and event queues. When debugging a production incident, it isn't always clear whether a problem exists in one system or another. This lack of specificity means metrics and logs only form a small part of the picture. Sometimes we need to zoom out and look at the complete life cycle of a request from the user agent to a terminal service and back again.

In 2010, engineers at Google published a paper describing **Dapper** (`https://research.google.com/archive/papers/dapper-2010-1.pdf`), a large-scale distributed systems tracing infrastructure. The paper described how Google had been using an internally developed tracing system to aid in observing system behavior and debugging performance issues. This work inspired others, including engineers at Twitter who, in 2012, introduced an open source distributed tracing system called **Zipkin** (`https://blog.twitter.com/engineering/en_us/a/2012/distributed-systems-tracing-with-zipkin.html`). Zipkin started out as an implementation of the Dapper paper but evolved into a full set of tools for analyzing performance and inspecting requests to Twitter infrastructure.

All of the work going on in the tracing space made apparent a need for some kind of standardized API. The **OpenTracing** (`http://opentracing.io/`) framework is an attempt to do just that. OpenTracing defines a specification detailing a pan-language standard for traces. Many engineers from different companies have contributed to this effort, including the engineers at Uber who originally created Jaeger (`https://eng.uber.com/distributed-tracing/`), an open source, end-to-end distributed tracing system that conforms to the OpenTracing specification.

In this recipe, we'll modify our message-service to add support for tracing. We'll then run Jaeger in a docker container so that we can see a few traces in practice.

How to do it...

1. Open the message-service project and replace the contents of `build.gradle` with the following:

```
group 'com.packtpub.microservices'
version '1.0-SNAPSHOT'

buildscript {
    repositories {
        mavenCentral()
    }
    dependencies {
        classpath group: 'org.springframework.boot', name: 'spring-
boot-gradle-plugin', version: '2.0.4.RELEASE'
    }
}

apply plugin: 'java'
apply plugin: 'org.springframework.boot'

sourceCompatibility = 1.8

repositories {
    mavenCentral()
}

dependencies {
    compile group: 'org.springframework.boot', name: 'spring-boot-
starter-web', version: '2.0.4.RELEASE'
    compile group: 'org.springframework.boot', name: 'spring-boot-
starter-actuator', version: '2.0.4.RELEASE'
    compile group: 'io.micrometer', name: 'micrometer-core',
version: '1.0.6'
    compile group: 'io.micrometer', name: 'micrometer-registry-
statsd', version: '1.0.6'
    compile group: 'io.opentracing.contrib', name: 'opentracing-
spring-cloud-starter-jaeger', version: '0.1.13'
    compile group: 'io.github.resilience4j', name: 'resilience4j-
circuitbreaker', version: '0.11.0'
    compile group: 'log4j', name: 'log4j', version: '1.2.17'
    compile group: 'net.logstash.logback', name: 'logstash-logback-
```

```
encoder', version: '5.2'
    testCompile group: 'junit', name: 'junit', version: '4.12'
}
```

2. Open `application.yml` in the `src/main/resources` directory and add a section for `opentracing` configuration. Here we're configuring our `opentracing` implementation to connect to an instance of Jaeger running locally on port `6831`:

```
opentracing:
  jaeger:
    udp-sender:
      host: "localhost"
      port:
        6831

spring:
  application:
    name: "message-service"
```

3. In order to collect traces, we'll run an instance of Jaeger locally. Docker makes this easy with the following command:

```
docker run -d --name jaeger \
  -e COLLECTOR_ZIPKIN_HTTP_PORT=9411 \
  -p 5775:5775/udp \
  -p 6831:6831/udp \
  -p 6832:6832/udp \
  -p 5778:5778 \
  -p 16686:16686 \
  -p 14268:14268 \
  -p 9411:9411 \
  jaegertracing/all-in-one:latest
```

4. Run message-service and make a few example requests (even if they result in a 404). Open `http://localhost:16686` in your browser and you'll see Jaeger's web UI. Hit search and explore the trace data collected so far!

Alerting us when something goes wrong

If you're seriously looking at microservices, you're probably running a 24/7 service. Customers demand that your service is available to use at any time. Contrast this increase in the need for availability with the reality that distributed systems are constantly experiencing some kind of failure. No system is ever completely healthy.

Whether you have a monolith or microservices architecture, it is pointless to try to avoid production incidents altogether. Instead, you should try to optimize how you are able to respond to failures, limiting their impact on customers by reducing the time it takes to resolve them.

Reducing the time it takes to resolve incidents (often measured as mean time to resolve or MTTR) involves first reducing the **Mean Time To Detect** (**MTTD**). Being able to accurately alert the right on-call engineer when a service is in a customer-impacting failure state is paramount to being able to maintain uptime. Good alerts should be actionable and urgent; if your system notifies on-call engineers when failures are either unactionable or non-urgent (not customer-impacting), you risk burning out on-call engineers and creating what is commonly referred to as alert fatigue. Alert fatigue is very real and can have a more catastrophic impact on uptime than any amount of software bugs or failing hardware. It is essential to continuously improve your system's alerting to get thresholds and other factors just right, to prevent false positives while maintaining alerting for truly customer-impacting incidents.

Alerting infrastructure is not something you want to build yourself. **PagerDuty** is an SaaS tool that allows you to create escalation policies and schedules for teams of engineers who are on-call for specific services. Using PagerDuty, you can set up a rotating schedule so that an engineer on a team of five, for example, can expect to be on-call one week in every five. Escalation policies allow you to configure a set of steps in case the on-call engineer is unavailable (perhaps they're driving their car on the freeway). Escalation policies are often configured to page a secondary on-call schedule, a manager, or even the entire team in the event that an incident goes unacknowledged for a certain amount of time. Using a system such as PagerDuty allows engineers on a team to enjoy much-needed off-call time while knowing that customer-impacting incidents will be responded to promptly.

Alerts can be configured manually using any number of supporting integrations, but this is time-consuming and error-prone. Instead, it's desirable to have a system that allows you to automate the creation and maintenance of alerts for your services. The Prometheus monitoring and alerting toolkit covered in this chapter includes a tool called Alertmanager which allows you to do just that. In this recipe, we'll modify our message-service to add alerts using Alertmanager. Specifically, we'll configure a single alert that fires when the average response time exceeds 500 ms for at least 5 minutes. We'll work from the version of message-service that already includes Prometheus metrics. We won't add any PagerDuty integration in this recipe, since that would require a PagerDuty account in order to follow along. PagerDuty has an excellent integration guide on its website. We'll configure `alertmanager` to send a simple WebHook-based alert.

How to do it...

Now, let's have a look at the following steps:

1. In a previous recipe, we configured Prometheus with a file called `prometheus.yml`. We'll need to add the `alertmanager` configuration to this file, so open it again and add the following:

```
# my global config
global:
  scrape_interval:     15s # Set the scrape interval to every 15
seconds. Default is every 1 minute.
  evaluation_interval: 15s # Evaluate rules every 15 seconds. The
default is every 1 minute.
  # scrape_timeout is set to the global default (10s).

# Alertmanager configuration
alerting:
  alertmanagers:
  - static_configs:
    - targets:
      - localhost:9093

# Load rules once and periodically evaluate them according to the
global 'evaluation_interval'.
rule_files:
  - "rules.yml"
  # - "first_rules.yml"
  # - "second_rules.yml"

# A scrape configuration containing exactly one endpoint to scrape:
# Here it's Prometheus itself.
scrape_configs:
  # The job name is added as a label `job=<job_name>` to any
timeseries scraped from this config.
  - job_name: 'prometheus'

    # metrics_path defaults to '/metrics'
    # scheme defaults to 'http'.

    static_configs:
    - targets: ['localhost:9090']

  - job_name: 'message-service'
    metrics_path: '/manage/prometheus'
    static_configs:
    - targets: ['localhost:8081']
```

2. Create a new file called `/tmp/rules.yml`. This file defines the rules we want Prometheus to be able to creates alerts for:

```yaml
groups:
- name: message-service-latency
  rules:
  - alert: HighLatency
    expr: rate(http_server_requests_seconds_sum{job="message-service", instance="localhost:8081"}[1m]) / rate(http_server_requests_seconds_count{job="message-service", instance="localhost:8081"}[1m]) > .5
    for: 1m
    labels:
      severity: 'critical'
    annotations:
      summary: High request latency
```

3. Create a new file called `/tmp/alertmanager.yml`. This is the file that will describe our alerting configuration. It is broken into a few different sections, global sets of certain configuration options that impact how `alertmanager` works. The section called receivers is where we configure our alert notification systems. In this case, it's a WebHook to a service running locally. This is just for demo purposes; we'll write a small ruby script that listens for HTTP requests and prints the payload to the standard output:

```yaml
global:
  resolve_timeout: 5m

route:
  group_by: ['alertname']
  group_wait: 10s
  group_interval: 10s
  repeat_interval: 1h
  receiver: 'web.hook'

receivers:
- name: 'web.hook'
  webhook_configs:
  - url: 'http://127.0.0.1:4567/'
```

4. Here's the source code for the small ruby service that will print out our alerts:

```ruby
require 'sinatra'

post '/' do
    body = request.body.read()
    puts body
    return body
end
```

5. Run the ruby script, restart `prometheus`, and start `alertmanager`. With these three systems running, we'll be ready to test our alert:

```
$ ruby echo.rb
...

$ ./prometheus --config.file=/tmp/prometheus.yml

$ ./alertmanager --config.file=/tmp/alertmanager.yml
...
```

6. In order to get our alert to fire, open message-service and add the following line to `MessageController.java`. It's a single line that will force the controller to sleep for 600 milliseconds before returning a response. Note that this is above our threshold described in our rules configuration:

```java
@RequestMapping(path = "/{id}", method = RequestMethod.GET,
produces = "application/json")
public Message get(@PathVariable("id") String id) throws
MessageNotFoundException {
    try { Thread.sleep(600); } catch (InterruptedException e) }
e.printStackTrace(); }
    return messagesStore.get(id);
}
```

7. With that in place, run your updated message service and make a number of requests to it. After one minute, Prometheus should notify Alertmanager, which should then notify your local debug ruby service. Your alert is working!

8
Scaling

In this chapter, we will cover the following recipes:

- Load testing microservices with Vegeta
- Load testing microservices with Gatling
- Building auto-scaling clusters

Introduction

A significant advantage of using microservices over a monolith architecture is that microservices can be separately scaled to meet the unique traffic demands they serve. A service that must do work for every single request will have very different scaling needs than a service that only needs to perform work for specific kinds of request.

Because microservices encapsulate ownership over a single-domain entity, they can be load tested independently. They can also be configured to scale automatically based on demand. In this chapter, we'll discuss load testing using two different load testing tools and set up auto-scaling groups in AWS that can scale on demand. Finally, we'll discuss strategies for capacity-planning.

Load testing microservices with Vegeta

Load testing is an important part of predicting how your service is going to behave over time. When we are performing load testing, we shouldn't just ask simple questions, such as "*How many requests per second is our system capable of serving?*" Instead, we should try to understand how our whole system performs under various load conditions. In order to answer this question, we need to understand the infrastructure that makes up our system and the dependencies that a particular service has.

For example, is the service behind a load-balancer? How about a CDN? What other caching mechanisms are used? All of these questions and more can be answered by our systems having good observability.

Vegeta is an open source load testing utility designed to test HTTP services with a constant request rate. It's a versatile tool that can be used as a command-line utility or a library. In this recipe, we'll focus on using the command-line utility. Vegeta allows you to specify targets as URLs in a separate file—optionally with custom headers and request bodies—that can be used as an input to the command-line tool. The command-line tool can then attack the targets in the file, with various options to control the request rate and duration, as well as other variables.

In this recipe, we'll be using Vegeta to test the message-service we've been working with in previous chapters. We'll test a simple request path that includes creating a new message and retrieving a list of messages.

How to do it...

Let's have a look at the following steps:

1. We'll modify our message-service and add a new endpoint that allows us to query all messages for a particular user. This introduces the notion of an inbox, so we'll modify our `MessageRepository` class to add a new in-memory map of usernames to lists of messages, as shown in the following code. Note that in a production system, we'd choose a more durable and flexible store, but this will suffice for demonstration purposes:

```
package com.packtpub.microservices.ch08.message;

import
com.packtpub.microservices.ch08.message.exceptions.MessageNotFoundE
xception;
import com.packtpub.microservices.ch08.message.models.Message;

import java.util.*;
import java.util.concurrent.ConcurrentHashMap;

public class MessageRepository {

    private ConcurrentHashMap<String, Message> messages;
    private ConcurrentHashMap<String, List<Message>> inbox;

    public MessageRepository() {
        messages = new ConcurrentHashMap<>();
```

```
        inbox = new ConcurrentHashMap<>();
    }

    public Message save(Message message) {
        UUID uuid = UUID.randomUUID();
        Message saved = new Message(uuid.toString(),
message.getSender(), message.getRecipient(),
                message.getBody(), message.getAttachmentUri());
        messages.put(uuid.toString(), saved);
        List<Message> userInbox =
inbox.getOrDefault(message.getRecipient(), new ArrayList<>());
        userInbox.add(saved);
        inbox.put(message.getRecipient(), userInbox);
        return saved;
    }

    public Message get(String id) throws MessageNotFoundException {
        if (messages.containsKey(id)) {
            return messages.get(id);
        } else {
            throw new MessageNotFoundException("Message " + id + "
could not be found");
        }
    }

    public List<Message> getByUser(String userId) {
        return inbox.getOrDefault(userId, new ArrayList<>());
    }
}
```

2. Modify `MessageController` to add the endpoint itself:

```
package com.packtpub.microservices.ch08.message.controllers;

import com.packtpub.microservices.ch08.message.MessageRepository;
import
com.packtpub.microservices.ch08.message.clients.SocialGraphClient;
import
com.packtpub.microservices.ch08.message.exceptions.MessageNotFoundE
xception;
import
com.packtpub.microservices.ch08.message.exceptions.MessageSendForbi
ddenException;
import
com.packtpub.microservices.ch08.message.exceptions.MessagesNotFound
Exception;
import com.packtpub.microservices.ch08.message.models.Message;
import
```

```
com.packtpub.microservices.ch08.message.models.UserFriendships;
import org.springframework.beans.factory.annotation.Autowired;
import org.springframework.http.ResponseEntity;
import org.springframework.scheduling.annotation.Async;
import org.springframework.web.bind.annotation.*;
import org.springframework.web.client.RestTemplate;
import
org.springframework.web.servlet.support.ServletUriComponentsBuilder
;

import java.net.URI;
import java.util.List;
import java.util.concurrent.CompletableFuture;

@RestController
public class MessageController {

    @Autowired
    private MessageRepository messagesStore;

    @Autowired
    private SocialGraphClient socialGraphClient;

    @RequestMapping(path = "/{id}", method = RequestMethod.GET,
produces = "application/json")
    public Message get(@PathVariable("id") String id) throws
MessageNotFoundException {
        return messagesStore.get(id);
    }

    @RequestMapping(path = "/", method = RequestMethod.POST,
produces = "application/json")
    public ResponseEntity<Message> send(@RequestBody Message
message) throws MessageSendForbiddenException {
        List<String> friendships =
socialGraphClient.getFriendships(message.getSender());

        if (!friendships.contains(message.getRecipient())) {
            throw new MessageSendForbiddenException("Must be
friends to send message");
        }

        Message saved = messagesStore.save(message);
        URI location = ServletUriComponentsBuilder
                .fromCurrentRequest().path("/{id}")
                .buildAndExpand(saved.getId()).toUri();
        return ResponseEntity.created(location).build();
    }
```

```
    @RequestMapping(path = "/user/{userId}", method =
RequestMethod.GET, produces = "application/json")
    public ResponseEntity<List<Message>>
getByUser(@PathVariable("userId") String userId) throws
MessageNotFoundException {
        List<Message> inbox = messagesStore.getByUser(userId);
        if (inbox.isEmpty()) {
            throw new MessageNotFoundException("No messages found
for user: " + userId);
        }
        return ResponseEntity.ok(inbox);
    }

    @Async
    public CompletableFuture<Boolean> isFollowing(String fromUser,
String toUser) {
        String url = String.format(
"http://localhost:4567/followings?user=%s&filter=%s",
                fromUser, toUser);

        RestTemplate template = new RestTemplate();
        UserFriendships followings = template.getForObject(url,
UserFriendships.class);

        return CompletableFuture.completedFuture(
                followings.getFriendships().isEmpty()
        );
    }
}
```

3. We'll need a mock socialgraph service, so create the following Ruby script in a file called `socialgraph.rb` and run it:

```
require 'sinatra'

get '/friendships/:user' do
    content_type :json
    {
        username: "user:32134",
        friendships: [
            "user:12345"
        ]
    }.to_json
end
```

4. Install `vegeta`. If you're on Mac OS X and have HomeBrew installed, you can just use the following:

```
$ brew update && brew install vegeta
```

5. Before we can launch an attach with `vegeta`, we'll need to create a `targets` file. The first request we'll make will create a message with the specified request body. The second request will get a list of messages by user ID. Create a file called `message-request-body.json`, as shown in the following code:

```
{
    "sender": "user:32134",
    "recipient": "user:12345",
    "body": "Hello there!",
    "attachment_uri": "http://foo.com/image.png"
}
```

6. Create another file called `targets.txt`, as shown in the following code:

```
POST http://localhost:8082/
Content-Type: application/json
@message-request-body.json

GET http://localhost:8082/user:12345
```

7. With both our message-service and our mock socialgraph service running, we're ready to load test these two services using the following code:

```
$ cat targets.txt| vegeta attack –duration=60s –rate=100 | vegeta
report –reporter=text

Requests       [total, rate]           6000, 100.01
Duration       [total, attack, wait]   1m0.004668981s,
59.99172349s, 12.945491ms
Latencies      [mean, 50, 95, 99, max] 10.683968ms, 5.598656ms,
35.108562ms, 98.290388ms, 425.186942ms
Bytes In       [total, mean]           667057195, 111176.20
Bytes Out      [total, mean]           420000, 70.00
Success        [ratio]                 99.80%
Status Codes   [code:count]            201:3000  500:12  200:2988
Error Set:
50
```

Experiment with different duration values and request rates to see how the behavior of the system changes. If you increase the rate to 1,000, what happens? Depending on hardware and other factors, it's possible that the single-threaded Ruby mock service will be overwhelmed and trip the circuit breaker we added to the message-service. This should change certain details, such as the success rate, so it's an important observation to make. What would happen if you load tested the mock Ruby service separately?

In this recipe, we load tested the message-service, which depends on the socialgraph service. Both services were running locally, which was necessary for demonstration purposes and gives us some insight into how the two systems behave. In a production system, it's vital to load test your services in production so that you include all of the infrastructure involved in serving requests (load balancers, caches, and so on). In a production system, you can also monitor dashboards and look for changes to how your system behaves under load conditions.

Load testing microservices with Gatling

Gatling is an open source load testing tool that allows users to script custom scenarios using a *Scala-based DSL*. Scenarios can go beyond simple straight path testing and involve multiple steps, even simulating user behavior, such as pauses and making decisions about how to proceed based on output in the test. Gatling can be used to automate the load testing of microservices or even browser-based web applications.

In the previous recipe, we used Vegeta to send a constant request rate to our message-service. Our request path created a new message and then retrieved all messages for a user. This method had the advantage of being able to test the response time of retrieving all messages for a user as the list of messages grew. Vegeta excels at this type of testing, but because it is fed attack targets from a static file, you cannot use Vegeta to build dynamic request paths based on the responses from previous requests.

Because Gatling uses a DSL to script load testing scenarios, it's possible to make a request, capture some element of the response, and use that output to make decisions about future requests. In this recipe, we'll use Gatling to script a load testing scenario that involves creating a message and then retrieving that specific message by its ID. This is a very different kind of test than what we did in the previous recipe, so it's a good opportunity to demonstrate the differences between Vegeta and Gatling.

How to do it...

Let's check the following steps:

1. Download `gatling` for your platform. Gatling is distributed as a ZIP bundle and is available for download at `https://gatling.io/download/`. Unzip the bundle into the directory of your choice:

```
$ unzip gatling-charts-highcharts-bundle-2.3.1-bundle.zip
...
$ cd gatling-charts-highcharts-bundle-2.3.1
```

2. Simulations for `gatling` are placed by default in the `user-files/simulations` directory. Create a new subdirectory called `messageservice` and a new file called `BasicSimulation.scala`. This is the file that contains the code that describes your scenario. In our scenario, we'll use the Gatling DSL to script a POST request to the create message endpoint followed by a GET request to the message endpoint, as shown in the following code:

```scala
package messageservice

import io.gatling.core.Predef._
import io.gatling.http.Predef._
import scala.concurrent.duration._

class BasicSimulation extends Simulation {

  val httpConf = http
    .baseURL("http://localhost:8082")
    .acceptHeader("application/json")

  val scn = scenario("Create a message")
    .exec(
      http("createMessage")
        .post("/")
        .header("Content-Type", "application/json")
        .body(StringBody("""{"sender": "user:32134", "recipient":
"user:12345", "body": "Hello there!", "attachment_uri":
"http://foo.com/image.png"}"""))
        .check(header(HttpHeaderNames.Location).saveAs("location"))

    )
    .pause(1)
    .exec(
      http("getMessage")
```

```
                .get("${location}")
        )

    setUp(scn.inject(atOnceUsers(50)).protocols(httpConf))
    }
```

3. Create the same mock Ruby service we used in the previous recipe and run it:

```ruby
require 'sinatra'

get '/friendships/:user' do
    content_type :json
    {
        username: "user:32134",
        friendships: [
            "user:12345"
        ]
    }.to_json
end
```

4. Run the Ruby mock service as well as our message-service. From the Gatling directory, launch Gatling by running bin/gatling.sh. You'll be prompted to select a simulation to run. Choose messageservice.BasicSimulation:

```
$ bin/gatling.sh
GATLING_HOME is set to /Users/posman/projects/microservices-
cookbook/chapter08/gatling-charts-highcharts-bundle-2.3.1
Choose a simulation number:
     [0] computerdatabase.BasicSimulation
     [1] computerdatabase.advanced.AdvancedSimulationStep01
     [2] computerdatabase.advanced.AdvancedSimulationStep02
     [3] computerdatabase.advanced.AdvancedSimulationStep03
     [4] computerdatabase.advanced.AdvancedSimulationStep04
     [5] computerdatabase.advanced.AdvancedSimulationStep05
     [6] messageservice.BasicSimulation
6
Select simulation id (default is 'basicsimulation'). Accepted
characters are a-z, A-Z, 0-9, - and _

Select run description (optional)

Simulation messageservice.BasicSimulation started...
..
```

5. The output will show some statistics about the results from the load test. Requests will be bucketed into under 800 ms, between 800 ms and 1,200 ms, and over 1,200 ms. A link to an HTML file will be displayed. Open it in a browser to see charts and other useful visualizations about your load test.

As we've seen in this recipe, Gatling offers a lot of flexibility in running load tests. With some clever scripting using the DSL, it's possible to more closely simulate production traffic by parsing log files and generating requests, making dynamic decisions based on latency, responses, or other elements of requests. Both Gatling and Vegeta are great load testing tools that you can use to explore how your systems operate under various load conditions.

Building auto-scaling clusters

With the advent of virtualization and the move to cloud-based infrastructure, applications can exist on elastic infrastructure designed to grow and shrink based on anticipated or measured traffic patterns. If your application experiences peak periods, you shouldn't have to provision full capacity during non-peak periods, wasting compute resources and money. From virtualization to containers and container schedulers, it's more and more common to have dynamic infrastructure that changes to accommodate the needs of your system.

Microservices are a natural fit for auto-scaling. Because we can scale separate parts of a system separately, it's easier to measure the scaling needs of a specific service and its dependencies.

There are many ways to create auto-scaling clusters. In the next chapter, we'll talk about container orchestration tools, but without skipping ahead, auto-scaling clusters can also be created in any cloud provider. In this recipe, we'll cover creating auto-scaling compute clusters using *Amazon Web Services*, particularly Amazon EC2 Auto Scaling. We'll create a cluster with multiple EC2 instances running our message-service behind an **Application Load Balancer** (**ALB**). We'll configure out cluster to automatically add instances based on CPU utilization.

How to do it...

Let's check the following steps:

1. This recipe requires an AWS account. If you do not already have an AWS account, create one at `https://aws.amazon.com/premiumsupport/knowledge-center/create-and-activate-aws-account/` and create a set of access keys at `https://docs.aws.amazon.com/general/latest/gr/managing-aws-access-keys.html`. Install the `aws cli` utility. If you're on OS X and have HomeBrew installed, this can be done with the following:

   ```
   $ brew install aws
   ```

2. Configure the `aws` command-line utility, entering the access key you created:

   ```
   $ aws configure
   ```

3. Create a launch configuration. Launch configurations are templates used by auto-scaling groups when creating new instances. In this case, we've chosen an Amazon AMI and `t2.nano` as our EC2 instance type (see `https://aws.amazon.com/ec2/instance-types/` for more details), as shown in the following code:

   ```
   $ aws autoscaling create-launch-configuration --launch-
   configuration-name message-service-launch-configuration --image-id
   ari-f606f39f --instance-type t2.nano
   ```

4. Create the actual auto-scaling group. Auto-scaling groups have configurable maximum and minimum sizes that specify how much the auto-scaling group can shrink or grow based on demand. In this case, we'll create an auto-scaling group with a minimum of 1 instance and a maximum of 5 instances, as shown in the following code:

   ```
   $ aws autoscaling create-auto-scaling-group --auto-scaling-group-
   name message-service-asg --launch-configuration-name message-
   service-launch-configuration --max-size 5 --min-size 1 --
   availability-zones "us-east-1a"
   ```

5. We want the instances in our auto-scaling group to be accessible behind a load balancer, so we'll create that now:

```
$ aws elb create-load-balancer --load-balancer-name message-
service-lb --listeners
"Protocol=HTTP,LoadBalancerPort=80,InstanceProtocol=HTTP,InstancePo
rt=8082" --availability-zones us-east-1a

{
    "DNSName": "message-service-lb-1741394248.us-
east-1.elb.amazonaws.com"
}
```

6. In order to automatically scale our auto-scaling group, we need to define a metric. Clusters can be scaled based on memory, CPU utilization, or request rate. In this case, we're going to configure our scaling policy to use CPU utilization. If CPU utilization hits a 20% average, our auto-scaling group will create more instances. Create a file called `config.json`:

```
{
  "TargetValue": 20.0,
  "PredefinedMetricSpecification":
    {
      "PredefinedMetricType": "ASGAverageCPUUtilization"
    }
}
```

7. Attach the scaling policy to our auto-scaling group.

```
$ aws autoscaling put-scaling-policy --policy-name cpu20 --auto-
scaling-group-name message-service-asg --policy-type
TargetTrackingScaling --target-tracking-configuration
file://config.json
```

Our auto-scaling group is now configured to grow when CPU utilization exceeds a 20% average. Launch configurations can also include bootstrapping steps for installing and configuring your service—typically with some kind of configuration-management tool, such as **Chef** or **Puppet**—or it can be configured to pull a Docker image from a private Docker repository.

Deploying Microservices

9

In this chapter, we'll cover the following recipes:

- Configuring your service to run in a container
- Running multi-container applications with Docker Compose
- Deploying your service on Kubernetes
- Test releases with canary deployments

Introduction

The way we deliver software to users has changed dramatically over the years. In the not too distant past, it was common to deploy to production by running a shell script on a collection of servers that pulled an update from some kind of source control repository. The problems with this approach are clear—scaling this out was difficult, bootstrapping servers was error prone, and deployments could easily get stuck in an undesired state, resulting in unpredictable experiences for users.

The advent of configuration management systems, such as **Chef** or **Puppet**, improved this situation somewhat. Instead of having custom bash scripts or commands that ran on remote servers, remote servers could be tagged with a kind of role that instructed them on how to configure and install software. The declarative style of automating configuration was better suited for large-scale software deployments. Server automation tools such as **Fabric** or **Capistrano** were also adopted; they sought to automate the process of pushing code to production, and are still very popular today for applications that do not run in containers.

Containers have revolutionized the way we deliver software. Containers allow developers to package their code with all the dependencies, including libraries, the runtime, OS tools, and configurations. This allows code to be delivered without the need to configure the host server, which dramatically simplifies the process by removing the number of moving pieces.

The process of shipping services in containers has been referred to as **immutable infrastructure**, because once an image is built, it isn't typically changed; instead, new versions of a service result in a new image being built.

Another big change in how software is deployed is the popularization of the twelve-factor methodology (`https://12factor.net/`). **Twelve-factor** (or **12f**, as it is commonly written) is a set of guidelines originally written by engineers at Heroku. At their core, twelve-factor apps are designed to be loosely coupled with their environment, resulting in services that can be used along with various logging tools, configuration systems, package management systems, and source control systems. Arguably, the most universally adopted concepts employed by twelve-factor apps are that the configuration is accessed through environment variables and logs are output to standard out. As we saw in the previous chapters, this is how we've integrated with systems such as Vault. These chapters are worth a read, but we've already been following many concepts described in twelve-factor so far in this book.

In this chapter, we'll be discussing containers, orchestration, and scheduling, and various methods for safely shipping changes to users. This is a very active topic, and new techniques are being improvised and discussed, but the recipes in this chapter should serve as a good starting point, especially if you're accustomed to deploying monoliths on virtual machines or bare metal servers.

Configuring your service to run in a container

As we know, services are made up of source code and configurations. A service written in Java, for instance, can be packaged as a **Java Archive (JAR)** file containing compiled class files in Java bytecode, as well as resources such as configuration and properties files. Once packaged, the JAR file can then be executed on any machine running a **Java Virtual Machine (JVM)**.

In order for this to work, however, the machine that we want to run our service on must have a JVM installed. Oftentimes, it must be a specific version of the JVM. Additionally, the machine might need to have some other utilities installed, or it might need access to a shared filesystem. While these are not parts of the service themselves, they do make up what we refer to as the runtime environment of the service.

Linux containers are a technology that allow developers to package an application or service with its complete runtime environment. Containers separate out the runtime for a particular application from the runtime of the host machine that the container is running on.

This makes applications more portable, making it easier to move a service from one environment to another. An engineer can run a service on their laptop, then move it into a preproduction environment, and then into production, without changing the container itself. Containers also allow you to easily run multiple services on the same machine, therefore allowing much more flexibility in how application architectures are deployed and providing opportunities for operational cost optimization.

Docker is a container runtime and set of tools that allows you to create self-contained execution environments for your service. There are other popular container runtimes they are widely used today, but Docker is designed to make containers portable and flexible, making it an ideal choice for building containers for services.

In this recipe, we'll use Docker to create an image that packages our message-service. We'll do this by creating a `Dockerfile` file and using the Docker command-line utility to create an image and then run that image as a container.

How to do it...

The steps for this recipe are as follows:

1. First, open our message-service project from the previous chapters. Create a new file in the root of the project called `Dockerfile`:

   ```
   FROM openjdk:8-jdk-alpine
   VOLUME /tmp
   EXPOSE 8082
   ARG JAR_FILE=build/libs/message-service-1.0-SNAPSHOT.jar
   ADD ${JAR_FILE} app.jar
   ENTRYPOINT ["java","-Djava.security.egd=file:/dev/./urandom","-jar","/app.jar"]
   ```

2. The `Dockerfile` file defines the base image that we'll use to build our message-service image. In this case, we're basing our image off of an Alpine Linux image with OpenJDK 8. Next, we expose the port that our service binds to and define how to run our service after it's packaged as a JAR file. We're now ready to use the `Dockerfile` file to build an image. This is done with the following command:

   ```
   $ docker build . -t message-service:0.1.1
   ```

3. You can verify that the preceding command worked by running `docker images` and seeing ours listed. Now we're ready to run the message service by executing our service in a container. This is done with the `docker run` command. We'll also give it a port mapping and specify the image that we want to use to run our service:

```
$ docker run -p 0.0.0.0:8082:8082 message-service:0.1.1
```

Running multi-container applications with Docker Compose

Services rarely run in isolation. A microservice usually connects to a data store of some kind, and could have other runtime dependencies. In order to work on a microservice, it's necessary to run it locally on a developer's machine. Requiring engineers to manually install and manage all the runtime dependencies of a service in order to work on a microservice would be impractical and time consuming. Instead, we need a way to automatically manage runtime service dependencies.

Containers have made services more portable by packaging the runtime environment and configuration with the application code as a shippable artifact. In order to maximize the benefits of using containers for local development, it would be great to be able to declare all the dependencies and run them in separate containers. This is what Docker Compose is designed to do.

Docker Compose uses a declarative YAML configuration file to determine how an application should be executed in multiple containers. This makes it easy to quickly start up a service, a database, and any other runtime dependencies of the service in a way that makes local development especially easy.

In this recipe, we'll follow some of the steps from the previous recipe to create a `Dockerfile` file for the authentication-service project. We'll then create a Docker Compose file that specifies MySQL as a dependency of the authentication-service. We'll then look at how to configure our project and run it locally with one container running our application and another running a database server.

How to do it...

For this recipe, you need to perform the following steps:

1. Open the authentication-service project and create a new file called `Dockerfile`:

```
FROM openjdk:8-jdk-alpine
VOLUME /tmp
EXPOSE 8082
ARG JAR_FILE=build/libs/authentication-service-1.0-SNAPSHOT.jar
ADD ${JAR_FILE} app.jar
ENTRYPOINT ["java","-Djava.security.egd=file:/dev/./urandom","-
jar","/app.jar"]
```

2. Docker Compose uses a file called `docker-compose.yml` to declare how containerized applications should be run:

```yaml
version: '3'
services:
  authentication:
    build: .
    ports:
     - "8081:8081"
    links:
      - docker-mysql
    environment:
      DATABASE_HOST: 'docker-mysql'
      DATABASE_USER: 'root'
      DATABASE_PASSWORD: 'root'
      DATABASE_NAME: 'user_credentials'
      DATABASE_PORT: 3306
  docker-mysql:
    ports:
      - "3306:3306"
    image: mysql
    restart: always
    environment:
      MYSQL_ROOT_PASSWORD: 'root'
      MYSQL_DATABASE: 'user_credentials'
      MYSQL_ROOT_HOST: '%'
```

3. As we'll be connecting to the MySQL server running in the `docker-mysql` container, we'll need to modify our authentication-service configuration to use that host when connecting to MySQL:

```
server:
  port: 8081

spring:
  jpa.hibernate.ddl-auto: create
  datasource.url: jdbc:mysql://docker-mysql:3306/user_credentials
  datasource.username: root
  datasource.password: root

hibernate.dialect: org.hibernate.dialect.MySQLInnoDBDialect

secretKey: supers3cr3t
```

4. You can now run the authentication-service and MySQL with the following:

```
$ docker-compose up
Starting authentication-service_docker-mysql_1 ...
```

5. That's it! The authentication-service should now be running locally in a container.

Deploying your service on Kubernetes

Containers make services portable by allowing you to package code, dependencies, and the runtime environment together in one artifact. Deploying containers is generally easier than deploying applications that do not run in containers. The host does not need to have any special configuration or state; it just needs to be able to execute the container runtime. The ability to deploy one or more containers on a single host gave rise to another challenge when managing production environments—scheduling and orchestrating containers to run on specific hosts and manage scaling.

Kubernetes is an open source container orchestration tool. It is responsible for scheduling, managing, and scaling your containerized applications. With Kubernetes, you do not need to worry about deploying your container to one or more specific hosts. Instead, you declare what resources your container needs and let Kubernetes decide how to do the work (what host the container runs on, what services it runs alongside, and so on). Kubernetes grew out of the **Borg paper** (https://research.google.com/pubs/pub43438.html), published by engineers at Google, which described how they managed services in Google's data centers using the Borg cluster manager.

Kubernetes was started by Google as an open source project in 2014 and has enjoyed widespread adoption by organizations deploying code in containers.

Installing and managing a Kubernetes cluster is beyond the scope of this book. Luckily, a project called **Minikube** allows you to easily run a single-node Kubernetes cluster on your development machine. Even though the cluster only has one node, the way you interface with Kubernetes when deploying your service is generally the same, so the steps here can be followed for any Kubernetes cluster.

In this recipe, we'll install Minikube, start a single-node Kubernetes cluster, and deploy the `message-service` command we've worked with in previous chapters. We'll use the Kubernetes CLI tool (`kubectl`) to interface with Minikube.

How to do it...

For this recipe, you need to go through the following steps:

1. In order to demonstrate how to deploy our service to a `kubernetes` cluster, we'll be using a tool called `minikube`. The `minikube` tool makes it easy to run a single-node `kubernetes` cluster on a VM that can be run on a laptop or development machine. Install `minikube`. On macOS X, you can use HomeBrew to do this:

   ```
   $ brew install minikube
   ```

2. We'll also be using the `kubernetes` CLI tools in this recipe, so install those. On macOS X, using HomeBrew, you can type as follows:

   ```
   $ brew install kubernetes-cli
   ```

3. Now we're ready to start our single-node `kubernetes` cluster. You can do this by running `minikube start`:

   ```
   $ minikube start
   Starting local Kubernetes v1.10.0 cluster...
   Starting VM...
   Getting VM IP address...
   Moving files into cluster...
   Setting up certs...
   Connecting to cluster...
   Setting up kubeconfig...
   Starting cluster components...
   Kubectl is now configured to use the cluster.
   Loading cached images from config file
   ```

4. Next, set the `minikube` cluster up as the default configuration for the `kubectl` CLI tool:

```
$ kubectl config use-context minikube
Switched to context "minikube".
```

5. Verify that everything is configured properly by running the `cluster-info` command:

```
$ kubectl cluster-info
Kubernetes master is running at https://192.168.99.100:8443
KubeDNS is running at
https://192.168.99.100:8443/api/v1/namespaces/kube-system/services/
kube-dns:dns/proxy
```

To further debug and diagnose cluster problems, use `kubectl cluster-info dump`.

6. You should now be able to launch the `kubernetes` dashboard in a browser:

```
$ minikube dashboard
Waiting, endpoint for service is not ready yet...
Opening kubernetes dashboard in default browser...
```

7. The `minikube` tool uses a number of environment variables to configure the CLI client. Evaluate the environment variables with the following command:

```
$ eval $(minikube docker-env)
```

8. Next, we'll build the docker image for our service using the `Dockerfile` file created in the previous recipe:

```
$ docker build -t message-service:0.1.1
```

9. Finally, run the `message-service` command on the `kubernetes` cluster, telling `kubectl` the correct image to use and the port to expose:

```
$ kubectl run message-service --image=message-service:0.1.1 --
port=8082 --image-pull-policy=Never
```

10. We can verify that the `message-service` command is running in the `kubernetes` cluster by listing the pods on the cluster:

```
$ kubectl get pods
NAME READY STATUS RESTARTS AGE
message-service-87d85dd58-svzmj 1/1 Running 0 3s
```

11. In order to access the `message-service` command, we'll need to expose it as a new service:

```
$ kubectl expose deployment message-service --type=LoadBalancer
service/message-service exposed
```

12. We can verify the previous command by listing services on the `kubernetes` services:

```
$ kubectl get services

NAME TYPE CLUSTER-IP EXTERNAL-IP PORT(S) AGE
kubernetes ClusterIP 10.96.0.1 <none> 443/TCP 59d
message-service LoadBalancer 10.105.73.177 <pending> 8082:30382/TCP
4s
```

13. The `minikube` tool has a convenient command for accessing a service running on the `kubernetes` cluster. Running the following command will list the URL that the `message-service` command is running on:

```
$ minikube service list message-service
|-------------|----------------------|----------------------------
|
| NAMESPACE | NAME | URL |
|-------------|----------------------|----------------------------
|
| default | kubernetes | No node port |
| default | message-service | http://192.168.99.100:30382 |
| kube-system | kube-dns | No node port |
| kube-system | kubernetes-dashboard | http://192.168.99.100:30000
|
|-------------|----------------------|----------------------------
|
```

14. Use `curl` to try and make a request against the service to verify that it's working. Congratulations! You've deployed the `message-service` command on `kubernetes`.

Test releases with canary deployments

Improvements in best practices for deploying have greatly improved the stability of deploys over the years. Automating the repeatable steps, standardizing the way our application interacts with the runtime environment, and packaging our application code with the runtime environment have all made deployments safer and easier than they used to be.

Introducing new code to a production environment is not without risk, however. All the techniques discussed in this chapter help prevent predictable mistakes, but they do nothing to prevent actual software bugs from negatively impacting users of the software we write. Canary deployment is a technique for reducing this risk and increasing confidence in new code that is being deployed to production.

With a canary deployment, you begin by shipping your code to a small percentage of production traffic. You can then monitor metrics, logs, traces, or whatever other tools allow you to observe how your software is working. Once you are confident that things are going as they should, you can gradually increase the percentage of traffic that receives your updated version until all production traffic is being served by the newest release of your service.

The term **canary deployment** comes from a technique that coal miners used to use to protect themselves from carbon monoxide or methane poisoning. By having a canary in the mine, the toxic gases would kill the canary before the miners, giving the miners an early warning sign that they should get out. Similarly, canary deployments allow us to expose a subset of users to risk without impacting the rest of the production environment. Thankfully, no animals have to be harmed when deploying code to production environments.

Canary deployments used to be very difficult to get right. Teams shipping software in this way usually had to come up with some kind of feature-toggling solution that would gate requests to certain versions of the application being deployed. Thankfully, containers have made this much easier, and Kubernetes has made it even more so.

In this recipe, we'll deploy an update to our `message-service` application using a canary deployment. As Kubernetes is able to pull images from a Docker container registry, we'll run a registry locally. Normally, you'd use a self-hosted registry or a service such as *Docker Hub* or *Google Container Registry*. First, we'll ensure that we have a stable version of the `message-service` command running in `minikube`, then we'll introduce an update and gradually roll it out to 100% traffic.

How to do it...

Go through the following steps to set up a canary deployment:

1. Open the `message-service` project we've worked on in the previous recipes. Add the following `Dockerfile` file to the root directory of the project:

```
FROM openjdk:8-jdk-alpine
VOLUME /tmp
EXPOSE 8082
ARG JAR_FILE=build/libs/message-service-1.0-SNAPSHOT.jar
ADD ${JAR_FILE} app.jar
ENTRYPOINT ["java","-Djava.security.egd=file:/dev/./urandom","-
jar","/app.jar"]
```

2. In order for Kubernetes to know whether the service is running, we need to add a liveness probe endpoint. Open the `MessageController.java` file and add a method to respond to GET requests at the `/ping` path:

```
package com.packtpub.microservices.ch09.message.controllers;

import com.packtpub.microservices.ch09.message.MessageRepository;
import
com.packtpub.microservices.ch09.message.clients.SocialGraphClient;
import
com.packtpub.microservices.ch09.message.exceptions.MessageNotFoundE
xception;
import
com.packtpub.microservices.ch09.message.exceptions.MessageSendForbi
ddenException;
import com.packtpub.microservices.ch09.message.models.Message;
import
com.packtpub.microservices.ch09.message.models.UserFriendships;
import org.springframework.beans.factory.annotation.Autowired;
import org.springframework.http.ResponseEntity;
import org.springframework.scheduling.annotation.Async;
import org.springframework.web.bind.annotation.*;
import org.springframework.web.client.RestTemplate;
import
org.springframework.web.servlet.support.ServletUriComponentsBuilder
;

import java.net.URI;
import java.util.List;
import java.util.concurrent.CompletableFuture;

@RestController
```

```
public class MessageController {

    @Autowired
    private MessageRepository messagesStore;

    @Autowired
    private SocialGraphClient socialGraphClient;

    @RequestMapping(path = "/{id}", method = RequestMethod.GET,
produces = "application/json")
    public Message get(@PathVariable("id") String id) throws
MessageNotFoundException {
        return messagesStore.get(id);
    }

    @RequestMapping(path = "/ping", method = RequestMethod.GET)
    public String readinessProbe() {
        return "ok";
    }

    @RequestMapping(path = "/", method = RequestMethod.POST,
produces = "application/json")
    public ResponseEntity<Message> send(@RequestBody Message
message) throws MessageSendForbiddenException {
        List<String> friendships =
socialGraphClient.getFriendships(message.getSender());

        if (!friendships.contains(message.getRecipient())) {
            throw new MessageSendForbiddenException("Must be
friends to send message");
        }

        Message saved = messagesStore.save(message);
        URI location = ServletUriComponentsBuilder
                .fromCurrentRequest().path("/{id}")
                .buildAndExpand(saved.getId()).toUri();
        return ResponseEntity.created(location).build();
    }

    @RequestMapping(path = "/user/{userId}", method =
RequestMethod.GET, produces = "application/json")
    public ResponseEntity<List<Message>>
getByUser(@PathVariable("userId") String userId) throws
MessageNotFoundException  {
        List<Message> inbox = messagesStore.getByUser(userId);
        if (inbox.isEmpty()) {
            throw new MessageNotFoundException("No messages found
for user: " + userId);
```

```
        }
        return ResponseEntity.ok(inbox);
    }

    @Async
    public CompletableFuture<Boolean> isFollowing(String fromUser,
String toUser) {
        String url = String.format(
"http://localhost:4567/followings?user=%s&filter=%s",
                fromUser, toUser);

        RestTemplate template = new RestTemplate();
        UserFriendships followings = template.getForObject(url,
UserFriendships.class);

        return CompletableFuture.completedFuture(
                followings.getFriendships().isEmpty()
        );
    }
}
```

3. Let's start our container registry on port 5000:

```
$ docker run -d -p 5000:5000 --restart=always --name registry
registry:2
```

4. As we're using a local repository that is not configured with a valid SSL cert, start `minikube` with the ability to pull from insecure repositories:

```
$ minikube start --insecure-registry 127.0.0.1
```

5. Build the `message-service` docker image, and then push the image to the local container registry with the following commands:

```
$ docker build . -t message-service:0.1.1
...
$ docker tag message-service:0.1.1 localhost:5000/message-service
...
$ docker push localhost:5000/message-service
```

6. A **Kubernetes Deployment** object describes the desired state for a pod and
ReplicaSet. In our deployment, we'll specify that we want three replicas of our
message-service pod running at all times, and we'll specify the liveness probe
that we created a few steps earlier. To create a deployment for our message-
service, create a file called deployment.yaml with the following contents:

```
apiVersion: extensions/v1beta1
kind: Deployment
metadata:
  name: message-service
spec:
  replicas: 3
  template:
    metadata:
      labels:
        app: "message-service"
        track: "stable"
    spec:
      containers:
        - name: "message-service"
          image: "localhost:5000/message-service"
          imagePullPolicy: IfNotPresent
          ports:
            - containerPort: 8082
          livenessProbe:
            httpGet:
              path: /ping
              port: 8082
              scheme: HTTP
            initialDelaySeconds: 10
            periodSeconds: 30
            timeoutSeconds: 1
```

7. Next, using kubectl, we'll create our deployment object:

```
$ kubectl create -f deployment.yaml
```

8. You can now verify that our deployment is live and that Kubernetes is creating
the pod replicas by running kubectl get pods:

```
$ kubectl get pods
```

9. Now that our application is running in Kubernetes, the next step is to create an update and roll it out to a subset of pods. First, we need to create a new docker image; in this case, we'll call it version 0.1.2 and push it to the local repository:

```
$ docker build . -t message-service:0.1.2
. . .
$ docker tag message-service:0.1.2 localhost:5000/message-service
$ docker push localhost:5000/message-service
```

10. We can now configure a deployment to run the newest version of our image before rolling it out to the rest of the pods.

Other Books You May Enjoy

If you enjoyed this book, you may be interested in these other books by Packt:

TypeScript Microservices
Parth Ghiya

ISBN: 978-1-78883-075-1

- Get acquainted with the fundamentals behind microservices.
- Explore the behavioral changes needed for moving from monolithic to microservices.
- Dive into reactive programming, TypeScript and Node.js to learn its fundamentals in microservices
- Understand and design a service gateway and service registry for your microservices.
- Maintain the state of microservice and handle dependencies.
- Perfect your microservice with unit testing and Integration testing
- Develop a microservice, secure it, deploy it, and then scale it

Microservice Patterns and Best Practices
Vinicius Feitosa Pacheco

ISBN: 978-1-78847-403-0

- How to break monolithic application into microservices
- Implement caching strategies, CQRS and event sourcing, and circuit breaker patterns
- Incorporate different microservice design patterns, such as shared data, aggregator, proxy, and chained
- Utilize consolidate testing patterns such as integration, signature, and monkey tests
- Secure microservices with JWT, API gateway, and single sign on
- Deploy microservices with continuous integration or delivery, Blue-Green deployment

Leave a review - let other readers know what you think

Please share your thoughts on this book with others by leaving a review on the site that you bought it from. If you purchased the book from Amazon, please leave us an honest review on this book's Amazon page. This is vital so that other potential readers can see and use your unbiased opinion to make purchasing decisions, we can understand what our customers think about our products, and our authors can see your feedback on the title that they have worked with Packt to create. It will only take a few minutes of your time, but is valuable to other potential customers, our authors, and Packt. Thank you!

Index

www.ingramcontent.com/pod-product-compliance
Lightning Source LLC
Chambersburg PA
CBHW080635060326
40690CB00021B/4937